Reasons to Be Hopeful

Published in 2023 by The School of Life
First published in the USA in 2023
930 High Road, London, N12 9RT

Copyright © The School of Life 2023

Designed and typeset by Dan Cottrell Studio
Printed in Latvia by Livonia Print

All rights reserved. This book is sold subject to the condition that it shall not be resold, lent, hired out or otherwise circulated without express prior consent of the publisher.

A proportion of this book has appeared online at www.theschooloflife.com/articles

Every effort has been made to contact the copyright holders of the material reproduced in this book. If any have been inadvertently overlooked, the publisher will be pleased to make restitution at the earliest opportunity.

The School of Life is a resource for helping us understand ourselves, for improving our relationships, our careers and our social lives – as well as for helping us find calm and get more out of our leisure hours. We do this through creating films, workshops, books, apps and gifts.

www.theschooloflife.com

ISBN 978-1-912891-89-4

10 9 8 7 6 5 4 3 2 1

MIX
Paper | Supporting responsible forestry
FSC® C002795

Reasons to Be Hopeful

What remains consoling,
inspiring and beautiful

The School of Life

Contents

Introduction ... 7

1. Reasons of Darkness ... 10
I. Suffering is normal ... 12
II. Our brains are not fit for purpose ... 20
III. It would have been better not to be born ... 28
IV. Love will injure us ... 36
V. The lust for vengeance is endemic ... 42
VI. We regret so much ... 48
VII. The advantages of sadness ... 54

2. Reasons of Detachment ... 62
I. We need perspective ... 64
II. The ultimate fate of humanity is not our business ... 74
III. If it all collapsed, we'd be fine, eventually ... 80
IV. The equality of eternity ... 84
V. Live in voluntary exile ... 90
VI. We have blessedly poor memories ... 96
VII. Much of what others believe is nonsense ... 100
VIII. Defiance ... 106
IX. This too shall pass ... 112
X. Dust to dust ... 118

3.	**Reasons of Light**	124
I.	There's still time to find joy	126
II.	Small pleasures	132
III.	The consolations of home	146
IV.	Friends	156
V.	The beauty of industry	164
VI.	Reasons that bypass reason	172
VII.	Affection rather than understanding	176
VIII.	Elsewhere	182
IX.	Wonder	188
X.	The promise of dawn	194
XI.	Good escapism	204
XII.	Acceptance	210
XIII.	Future reasons to be hopeful	218

Introduction

For most of our lives, we don't require anything as specific or formal as 'reasons' to be hopeful; we take being cheerful for granted. We rise out of bed with purpose and direction; we may be preoccupied by this or that challenge, but the business of existence as a whole is never in question.

Then there are other moods, more sombre and confused in nature, in which what we are doing on earth comes to seem like a far more doubtful and painful matter. An accumulation of reversals – some minor, others more severe – undermine our will to endure much longer; the automatic reflex of living escapes us. There seems no point in getting up, we have no will to eat, we fall into a reverie halfway through pouring a glass of water, there is nowhere we can think of travelling, there is no one we want to talk to. We go through the motions, but our spirit is elsewhere. The best way our society knows how to interpret matters is to label us 'depressed' and to offer us a variety of numbing medications in response.

In this sad state, we can no longer say why we should take the trouble to get dressed or shower, why we should go to work or utter a word – why, in fact, we should take another breath. None of it seems obvious in the slightest. We might look around us in the park – at parents with children, pensioners with their dogs, or planes crossing the sky – and wonder by what peculiar, deluded and mysterious forces the whole vainglorious show is kept in motion.

It's not that we necessarily have a conscious grasp of why we have a taste for life when we do feel purposeful and optimistic. We have our reasons, but we don't have any need to identify them; they are so much in our command and so numerous that we don't single them out. At these times, we think it's life itself we love, rather than paying homage to any singular set of ingredients – for example, our health or our friends, our good name or our prospects of promotion. But when despair strikes, we cannot be so casual about the things that have the capacity to buoy us up.

We must learn to think through rigorously what we had been accustomed to locating by reflex; we must go in careful search of reasons to be. We need to ask ourselves, in a way the blessed never have to, how we are going to get through the coming years, and why we should bother, given the pain involved. What follows is a tool to assist us in our search. It seeks to lay before us some reasons why, despite everything, we might continue with tomorrow. The tone of the first section is deliberately grim. To protest at the pessimism on display would be to miss valuable reasons to go on living, as it isn't always optimism that best cheers us. Our spirits can be sunk by the punishing impression that everyone else is content and that we are alone in our misery. Accordingly, there is relief to be felt in remembering that sadness is widespread and that there are reasons why life is often hellish. We may be more effectively encouraged by a reminder that humanity is doomed, happiness is a mirage and the search for career success is absurd than by an invitation to appreciate spring flowers or to delight in bucolic art. Dark ideas can legitimately count as 'good' reasons to be hopeful when they diminish our sense of having been singled out for chastisement or condemned to suffer in isolation. They can reveal that our misery has always been, in reality, normal.

After a rendition of bitter truths, we move on to thoughts that restore perspective and situate our woes in a larger context of time and space. Finally, we shift to positive pleasures that, like the caress of morning light on the convalescent's cheek, await the recovering melancholic. There is room for soft cheese, a walk with a friend and early summer mornings in a list of reasons why we should not, after all, end matters right now. If we are to make a sustained recovery, we must work our way towards a personal, well-defined list of arguments for pushing back against the forces of forlornness. The makings of that list begin here.

1.

Reasons of Darkness

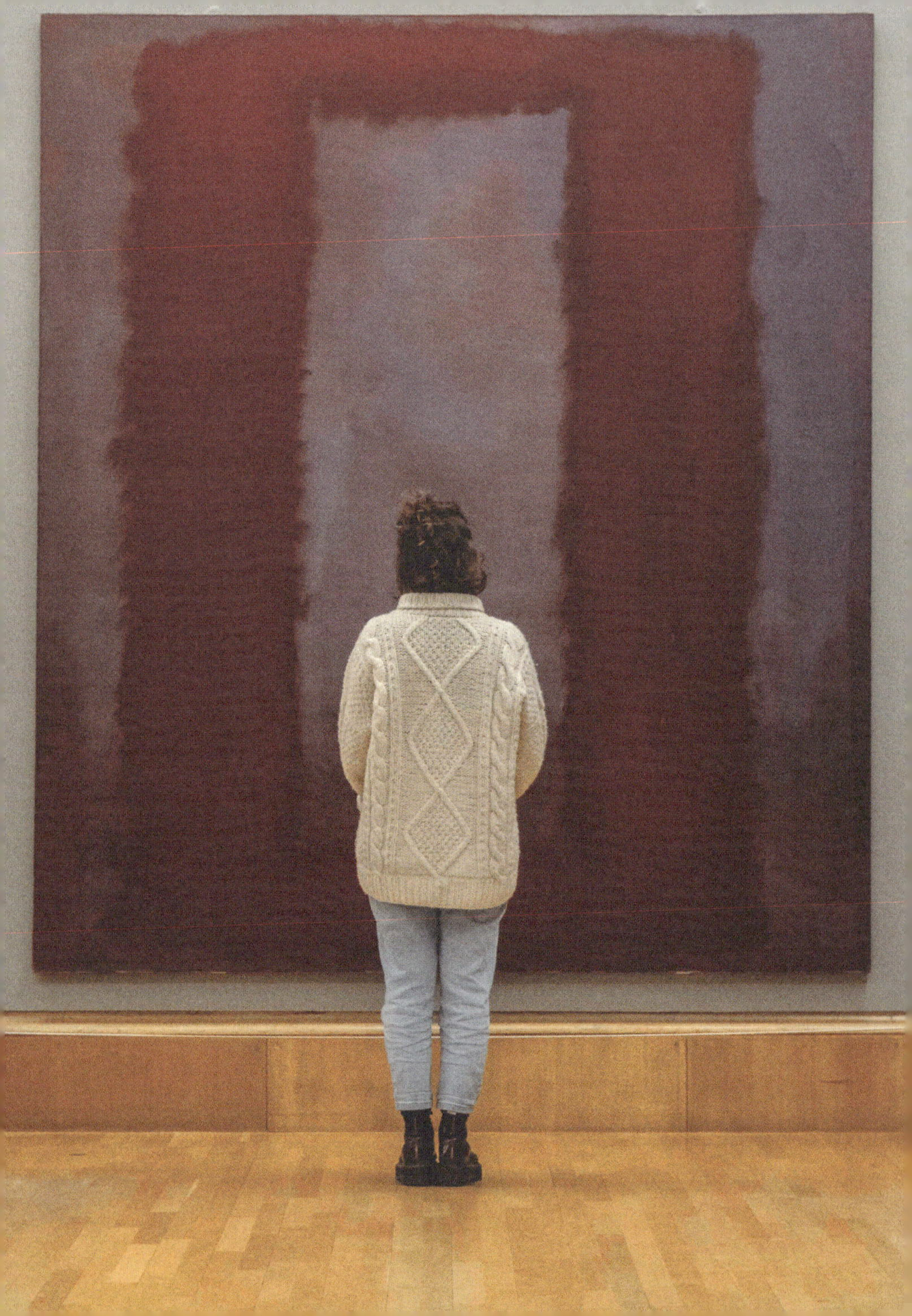

I.

Suffering is normal

Mark Rothko, *Red on Maroon*, from the Seagram Mural series, 1959. Rothko's canvases, though focused on darkness, lend our difficulties dignity and legitimacy.

Mark Rothko and the Seagram Murals

The most unexpectedly uplifting and consoling artist of the 20th century was the abstract painter Mark Rothko, the high priest of grief and loss who spent the latter part of his career turning out sublime and sombre canvases that spoke, as he put it, of the 'tragedy of being human' – and who, in 1970 at the age of 66, took his own life at his studio in New York.

Born in Dvinsk, Russia (now Daugavpils, Latvia), Rothko emigrated to the United States at the age of 10 and immediately grew wary of the aggressive good cheer and commercialism of his adopted land. He was a latter-day Leopardi or Pascal adrift in Disney World. Appalled by the sentimentality around him, he learnt to make art that was insular, unrelenting, sombre and oriented towards pain.

In 1958, Rothko was offered a large sum to paint some murals for an opulent, soon-to-be-opened New York restaurant, the Four Seasons on Park Avenue. Rothko described it to John Fischer, the editor of *Harper's Magazine*, as 'a place where the richest bastards of New York will come to feed and show off'. His intentions for the murals soon became clear: 'I hope to ruin the appetite of every son of a bitch who ever eats in that room'. And to that end,

Mark Rothko, *Red on Maroon*, 1959

he set to work on large black and maroon colour fields expressing a mood of terror and archaic anguish; by the time of the Seagram commission, Rothko's favourite colours were burgundy, dark grey, pitch black and burnt red, although still often punctuated by the decidedly brighter tones characteristic of his work in the 1940s and 50s.

It was an unlikely commission for Rothko to have accepted, but it became ever more so in his mind when, in the autumn of 1959 following a trip to Italy (where he had been much moved by Giotto's renditions of the Crucifixion), he took his wife Mell to the restaurant for lunch. His contempt became overwhelming. Believing it was 'criminal to spend more than $5 on a meal', he couldn't get over the overpriced dishes, the fancy sauces and the ponderous waiting staff. 'Anybody who will eat that kind of food for those kinds of prices will never look at a painting of mine,' he told one of his studio assistants. Rothko hated the Four Seasons' clientele: suntanned, cheery, rich people, out to celebrate and show themselves off, to cut deals and swap gossip. The apparent winners of life; the kind who invested in tennis lessons and whitened their teeth. His disdain had its roots in a sense that we only accede to our humanity when we face pain and commune around it with compassion and humility. Anything else is grandstanding and pride. He had remained Russian in his soul.

Following the lunch, Rothko called up his patrons, explained his feelings and sent back the money. He then gave his paintings to London's Tate gallery, where they were hung in a quiet, contemplative, religious-like space that enclosed the viewer in an atmosphere of meditative mortification. The paintings remain ideal companions for visitors who drift into the gallery at their wits' end, who might be working through the loss of a partner or the ruin of their career, and who need more than anything else to know that they are not alone.

Rothko's canvases, though focused on the darkness, are never themselves depressing to look at because they lend our difficulties dignity and legitimacy. To bathe in their atmosphere is to gain a distinct sense of comfort, like lying in the arms of a tender friend who says little more than a modest 'I know' in response to our dejection and loss. With Rothko as our guide, it matters a little less that the world is mostly filled with noisy, brash apparent winners, that no one much cares for us, that we have failed in countless ways, that our name isn't in lights, that we have enemies or that we are no longer young. We are offered a refuge from the boosterish voices of contemporary society, finding works that echo in an external form our own confused and inchoate sorrows.

A great part of our misery is caused by the cruel and erroneous assumption that life might fundamentally be a pleasant journey, capable of delivering satisfaction and delight to those who work hard and retain noble and purposeful hearts. The truth could not be further from such a sentimental vision. Agony is baked into the human condition. We suffer not by coincidence but by necessity. We may focus on the specific errors and cruelties that have brought us to a low point; we may be narrowly concerned with what our enemies have done to us, how a few mistakes have cost us everything or how we have been abandoned by those who should have cared for us. But to insist that these problems are merely local manifestations of more global and endemic troubles is not to minimise them. They are the specific mechanisms by which we have come to taste the sorrow that is the grisly birthright of every human, and which would have been our lot however fate had chosen to twist our path. Ultimately, we must all drink this poisoned liquid from the cup of sorrow, even if in different gulps and at different times. No one gets through unscathed.

Yet not only are we sad, we are isolated and lonely with our sadness. The official narrative is remorselessly upbeat and insists that we can find the right partner, that work can deliver satisfaction, that destinies are fair and that there is no inherent reason for us to lament our state. But we don't deserve to be forced to grin. We should be allowed to weep without being hectored into positivity. Our true right is not the right to happiness; it is the right to be miserable.

This may not sound like a reason to be hopeful, but the ability to look darkness in the face and accept its role in our affairs functions as its own very particular and intense reward. No longer must we be surprised by our suffering. No longer must we be taken unawares by misery. No longer do we have to feel that our reversals say something unique and shocking about us. Instead, we can start to rediscover a taste for life when we can see that we're not alone in wanting to give up on it; that it is acceptable – even necessary – to hate the smiling 'bastards' who so angered Rothko, and who would elicit a similar response from anyone else with a heart. We can build friendships around a shared honesty about tragedy. We will have banked our first reason to be hopeful when we recognise that we are not exceptionally stupid for finding things difficult. Unhappiness is, as wise artists have always liked to remind us (despite the suggestions of adverts, magazines and those seemingly confident people congratulating themselves in fancy restaurants), in fact, very normal indeed.

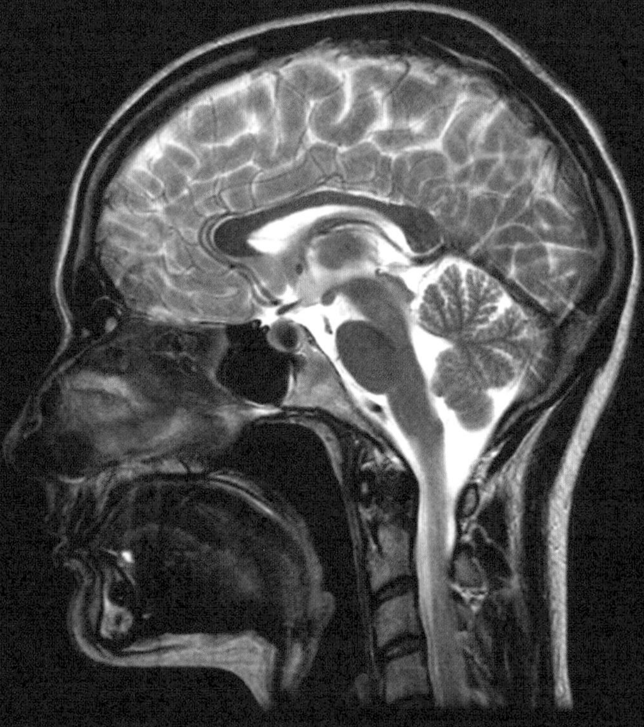

II.

Our brains are not fit for purpose

An MRI scan showing the structure of the brain, an organ with incredible ability yet wholly uninclined to think logically through its dilemmas.

MRI and the brain scan

Two photographs deserve to be counted as among the most significant of the 20th century. The first was taken on 24th December 1968 by the astronaut William Anders as the *Apollo 8* spacecraft orbited the Moon. It pictured the Earth as the legendary pale blue dot in an infinity of emptiness. The second image – far less well known – was taken in 1978 by a team of scientists led by Hugh Clow and Ian Robert Young at EMI Laboratories in England. This image revealed a cross-section of the human brain as seen through a magnetic resonance imaging (MRI) scanner.

MRI technology proved to be a revolutionary advance on the computed tomography (CT) scans that had preceded it, because it created brilliant contrasts, displaying areas that were high in water and fat in white, and those low in water and fat in black. MRI scans granted near-perfect vision of parts of the brain that had previously been known only from an anatomist's slab: the cerebellar cortex, the occipital lobe, the hypothalamus and the corpus callosum.

MRI gave our species a new degree of insight into itself. Everything that *Homo sapiens* had ever done, thought about, dreamt, imagined; every act of love, bitterness, vengeance, generosity and wonder had passed through this biological instrument, now resplendently displayed against the scan's cosmic darkness. This is what it looked like inside the craniums of our ancestors who crossed the Torres Strait, who colonised the Mongolian steppes, who guarded Jesus, who wrote the Magna Carta, who defended the last remaining Aztec temple, who cracked the Rosetta Stone and who invented the bikini.

But, after we have been awed as much as we can be by this extraordinary watery bundle – this 15-centimetre-long, 1.3-kilogram device, packed with 86 billion neurons; the simultaneous creator and interpreter of what we call reality – we can admit that this machine nevertheless presents us with as many problems as it does solutions.

Despite years of patient education and encouragement, this organ is wholly uninclined to think logically through its dilemmas. It is primarily an instrument of instinct; substantial portions of its lower basal folds operate with the rabid ferocity of those of a lizard or a rat. It responds at lightning speed to threats and lures with impulses honed over a 200,000-year history, but it is entirely reluctant to stay still for a while, pull out a pen and paper and analyse its feelings and desires with anything resembling rigour. The brain jumps into marriages, fires off hasty emails, starts lawsuits, places its hand on others' knees, blurts out its rage, stuffs itself with sugar and makes accusations – thereby repeatedly destroying the foundations of earthly contentment. All the calm and forethought, the perspective and resilience, that we would need to steer us through our difficulties are missing from this organic structure. Our wars and slums are visible from outer space; this is where they have their origins.

Sadly, this soupy walnut cannot recognise its worst proclivities and take protective measures against them. It might be around for fifty years before it comes to basic realisations about its workings: how much it gets wrong, what it misses, where it exaggerates, what it underplays, how others are likely to see it. A stranger can know more about it in a matter of minutes than its owners ascertain in decades. We are aware of only a tiny proportion of the ideas and drives that course through us. At rare moments – perhaps when falling asleep or waking up at an unusual hour – we get a hint of how much there is in our minds that we cannot properly touch; how many stray memories and bittersweet recollections swirl in the lower reaches of consciousness. Nothing quite disappears, nothing ever leaves us fully alone. We are filled with ghosts.

More pointedly, the machine is affected by events in its past that gravely distort its assessment of the present.

It may come to distrust all men or all women because a few examples once caused it harm. It may lose all ability to smile and be hopeful because it was attacked in its third year or harshly spoken to over its initial decade. It might expect that everyone will be mean to it because at a formative stage one or two people were. It can develop a conviction that it is unworthy and should be extinguished, or may be tempted to sabotage itself at its moments of greatest triumph. It can run away from kindly people because of a conviction that it doesn't deserve anything but hurt.

The mind is lazy, too. It can't work up the energy to interrogate itself on its wishes or put in motion plans that could nimbly realise them. It craves distraction just when it brushes up against important ideas. Only one in 10 million minds delivers on its true potential; what we call 'genius' is the rare will to faithfully transcribe the ideas that normally refuse to be pinned down, even though the raw ingredients for such ideas are present in everyone. We are almost certain to die having mined only a fraction of who we are.

When the mind falls seriously ill, there is almost nothing to be done. Our science is stuck at the level of medieval dentistry. Somewhere in the folds of our cortexes, out of reach of medicines and therapies, lie compulsions to despair, to refuse help, to injure ourselves and to remain addicted; we grow convinced of the worst plots and vendettas, and after years of suffering we may see no alternative but to fire a bullet through our own cerebral tissue.

So, though a technical and artistic triumph, a picture of the inside of our minds might be better greeted with ambivalence. We see at once the creation that underpins our most majestic moments and a piece of unreliable matter that keeps us mired in conflict, sadness and anger and is incapable of doing justice to our underlying brilliance.

The real response to this image should be compassion. We must do so much with a tool that is at best only half-fit for the task. With this piece of cobbled-together, intermittent, bug-filled hardware, we have to decide whom we should trust, what we should put our faith in, how we can manage our desires and what course of action we should follow. In another million years, we will have evolved out of the constraints of this particular model and we will look at it with the same pity as we do the first computers or the ill-adapted fins of early sea creatures. We will at last have minds that can help us to accomplish what we actually need from them – that won't just throw up mirages of happiness to tantalise us and then step back and watch us stray and stumble, but will be kind and nimble enough to navigate us through the darkness we actually face.

It is likely that we are already experts in self-flagellation; masters at itemising the many ways in which we are despicable, undeserving and shameful. After we have run through every argument about why we are so ignoble and daft, we should spare a moment to consider that the fault does not lie with us alone. Nature equipped us especially badly for the tasks we were obliged to take on, so we never had much of a chance. We were never granted the sort of brains we need in order not to suffer.

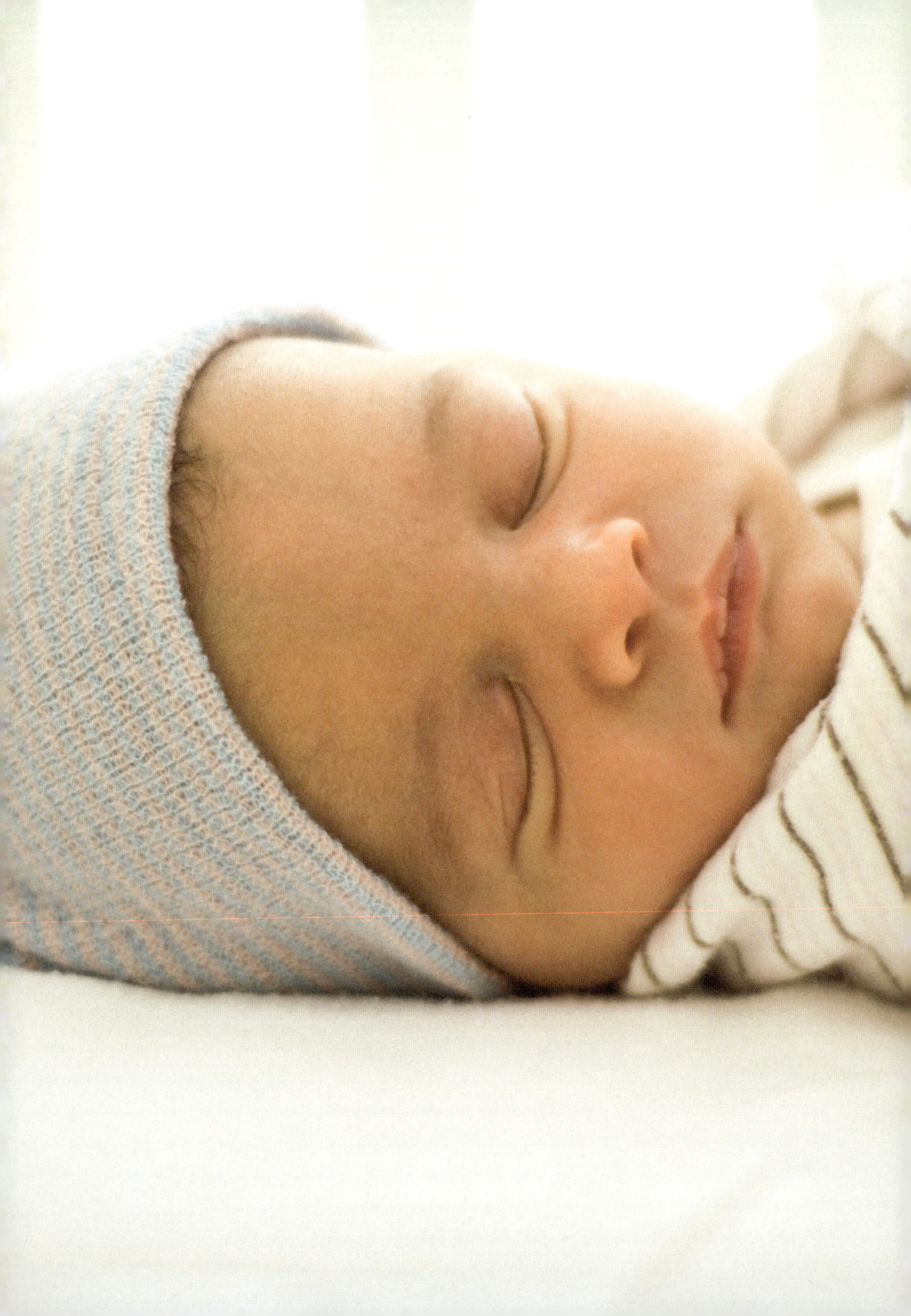

III.

It would have been better not to be born

There are many reasons to be concerned by the beauty and perfection of a sleeping baby.

The earliest days in the cot

It is common, on meeting with one of these tightly wrapped packages with a bonnet on its head, to marvel at the exceptional beauty and perfection on display. We look at the tightly closed eyes and wonder what mysterious regions this wizard might be travelling through in its mind. It seems at once to know nothing and everything, as if it contains within itself a trace of the wisdom of all ages; it looks both terribly young and infinitely old, totally naïve and boundlessly knowledgeable. It has been pulled as if by magic out of the realm of slumbering souls, having existed only a few months before as scattered atoms that might have reached the Earth from exploding stars in the early days of the universe. Now it has taken shape as a unique being, with neat, folded eyelids and a soft downy head, that might live for only 100 years.

We may be moved, but at the same time there are many reasons to be extremely concerned. Our young friend is preparing to enter a world that ravages all who have ever been impudent enough to step into it – a world in which its own needs and wants will not figure highly on any stranger's list of concerns and in which it will soon enough be told to grow up and stop pitying itself. It will have to earn its keep by competing ruthlessly with its peers, those it loves will seldom love it back as intently as it longs for, it will be the target of envy and backbiting, it will struggle to understand itself and it will mess up key decisions. It is entering a place where it will never again enjoy the peace and comfort of those early, tightly swaddled days.

Before it can truly rest once more, this brave warrior's heart will beat some 4 billion times, it will be humiliated, it will be ignored, it will want to die, it will cry out in agony and feel forsaken. It will lie awake in lonely hotel rooms, terrified of what the future will bring, or toss and turn next to someone it wants to separate from but acutely doesn't want to hurt. It will write imploring letters to people begging for mercy. It will knock at the doors of loved ones who don't want to answer. It will struggle to make itself understood by family members. It will have to drag itself out of bed for a job that crushes its spirit. It will have arguments with spouses who are in no mood to see things from its point of view. It will feel nostalgic for its younger self and remember with bittersweetness its promising beginnings that so starkly illuminate its later disappointments: the badges it won at school, the excitement at the end of its exams, those early summers by the beach.

Its parents are likely to want this little life to go extremely well, but how little agency they ultimately possess against the multiple horrors waiting outside the nursery door, how often they will have to stand back helplessly and watch as fate does its worst. For a few years, they can make sure that there is a kiss every evening, that the lunchbox is filled with apple slices and the favourite tuna sandwiches and that there is help with homework and tying shoelaces. But soon enough, the child will have to make its way unaided and there will be no chance to stop the blows or the tears.

There is much art in the Christian tradition depicting mothers and babies. Unlike the modern rigmarole concerning children, this religious art stands out for bathing both parent and child in an atmosphere of sadness. In a typical altarpiece, a thoughtful Jesus sits on Mary's lap, gazing upwards, playing with her hair or looking at the pages of a holy book while she looks down at him or into the distance with an air of deep melancholy. Mary seems to be under no illusions about what life has in store – she senses that this child won't get through without agony. Her love for him is a source of terrible pain because his suffering will automatically become hers. Already in the nursery there is an apprehension of the martyrdom on Calvary. Life is a gift to be celebrated and, at the same time, an unmitigated tragedy. That, these paintings tell us, is the lot of humankind.

Rogier van der Weyden, *The Virgin and Child*, 1435–1438

We may not be headed for a crucifixion outside Jerusalem, but – as the Christian story makes clear – we will all suffer in ways that lack justice or proportion and that will leave any loving parent distressed and terrified. We have done nothing wrong but been born, and yet that will be enough to merit ample, devilish punishment.

The ancient Greek historian Herodotus observed with approval that the Thracian peoples were in the habit of celebrating at funerals and, conversely, of weeping at births. If we were more clear-eyed, or simply less taken in by the smiles of young ones, we might have the courage to follow these sombre realists in their prescient lamentations.

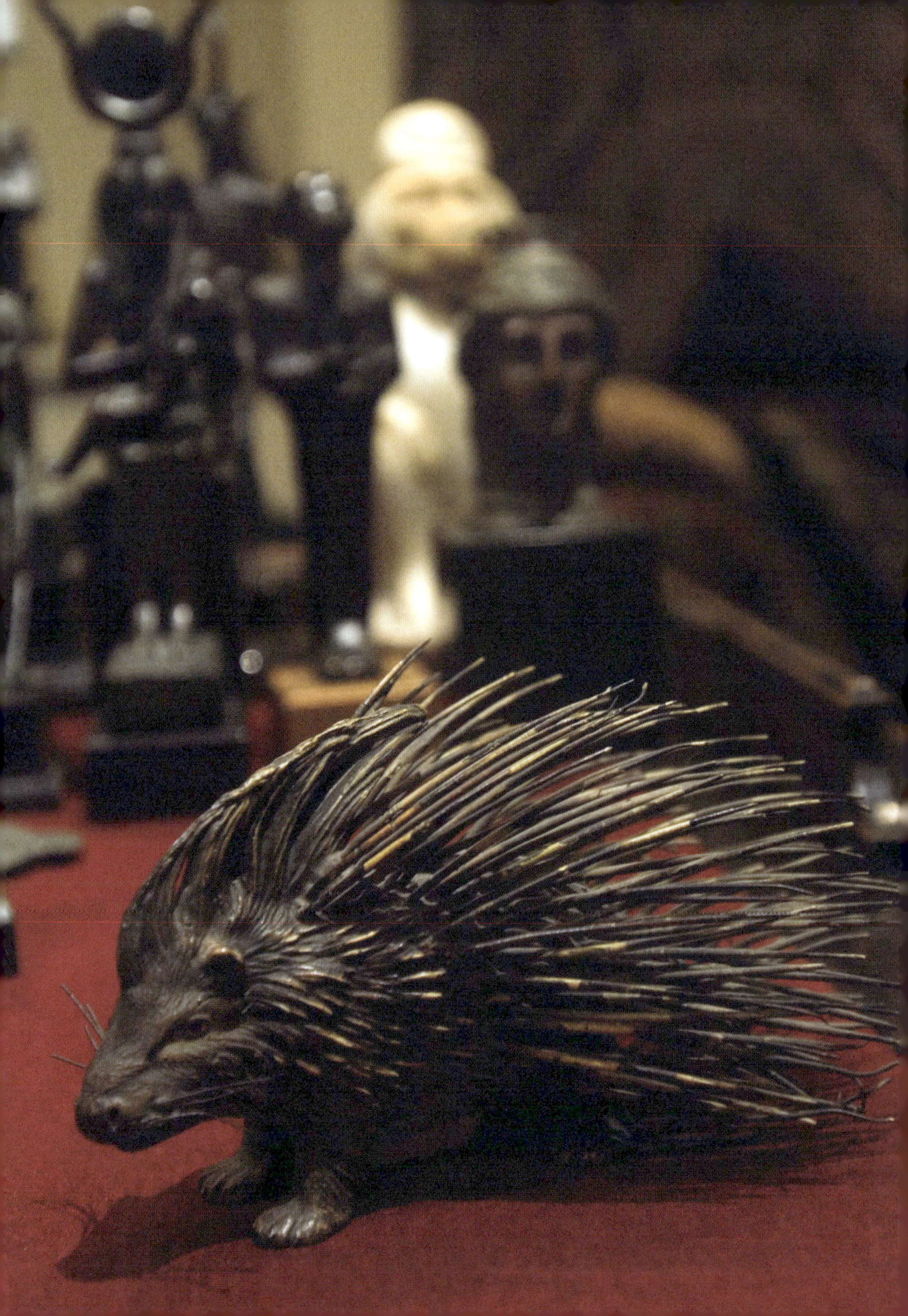

IV.

Love will injure us

A bronze model of a porcupine on Sigmund Freud's desk.
The porcupine represents the human capacity to hurt those we are close to.

Freud's unhappy porcupines

We know what love should be like. We imagine our desired partners long before we meet them in real life – they will be kind, beautiful, gentle, thoughtful, inspiring and funny. They will be infinitely careful with the precious, vulnerable sides of us, and we with theirs. They will be our refuge and our home.

Through all the difficulties and tragicomic ordeals of our romantic quests – the absurdities and puzzles of dating, the broken relationships, the fractious marriages, the unsatisfactory affairs – we keep them in mind. We mock this or that failed candidate or demented or evil partner, but we never dare to mock love itself; we never question what we're trying to do, but rather insist that we haven't yet met 'the right person' to do it with.

It would be wise to take advantage of our sad mood and dare to be braver. We have met plenty of people and we have had many opportunities to make things work. Our ongoing travails aren't a sign that we need to try out yet more candidates; they are evidence that what we long for in love and what other people can plausibly deliver are fundamentally opposed.

Porcupines are herbivorous rodents covered in sharp quills, with only a thin layer of subcutaneous fat to keep them warm. On chilly nights, they must huddle together in burrows with other members of their species – but in doing so, they often badly injure themselves against the quills of their neighbours. It isn't uncommon to see porcupines stumbling out of the ground at dawn with traces of blood across their bodies. The rodents buy their protection at a high cost: it is a choice between hypothermia and injury.

Sigmund Freud thought a lot about porcupines, and in tribute to their perplexities around intimacy, he placed a bronze model of one on his desk, first in Vienna and later in London, where it remains to this day.

As his patients detailed their struggles – wives who felt unloved, husbands who could not be faithful, partners who did not hear each other's complaints, seducers who could only desire when they were rejected – Freud could look over at the razor-sharp bronze quills and know that what he was hearing were not isolated cases of unhappiness, but further examples of the risks we encounter whenever we seek a necessary alternative to our own company.

Freud's psychoanalytic practice went on to establish an unparalleled understanding of why we are so prone to bloodying ourselves in relationships. Each of us arrives in adulthood with a history that militates against our chances of present-day contentment. The early weeks of passion may go well enough, but our complicated pasts soon make themselves felt. Perhaps, as children, we were made to feel worthless and ashamed, so now the love of another person will seem unreal and in need of constant challenge. Or, because our childhoods left us anxious about the unreliability of others, we continually demand reassurance and signs of loyalty, which eventually drives away the very person we are so keen to keep close. We may look sweet, we may have our kindly moments and we are not always perturbed, but sure enough, each one of us is covered in quills that will jab and gravely injure anyone reckless enough to come close to us.

As a species, we spend far too long regretting our specific choices, and far too little time gaining melancholy comfort from the knowledge that intimacy is rendered inherently and impossibly problematic by our jagged psyches.

The very best candidates won't be the ones who don't hurt us – they don't exist. They will be those who at least have some sense of how they will do so, and as such can warn us of the fact in good time, with grace and a touch of humour. We should, on our early dinner dates, learn to turn to a prospective porcupine and ask with a melancholy smile: 'So how might you jab me with your quills?'

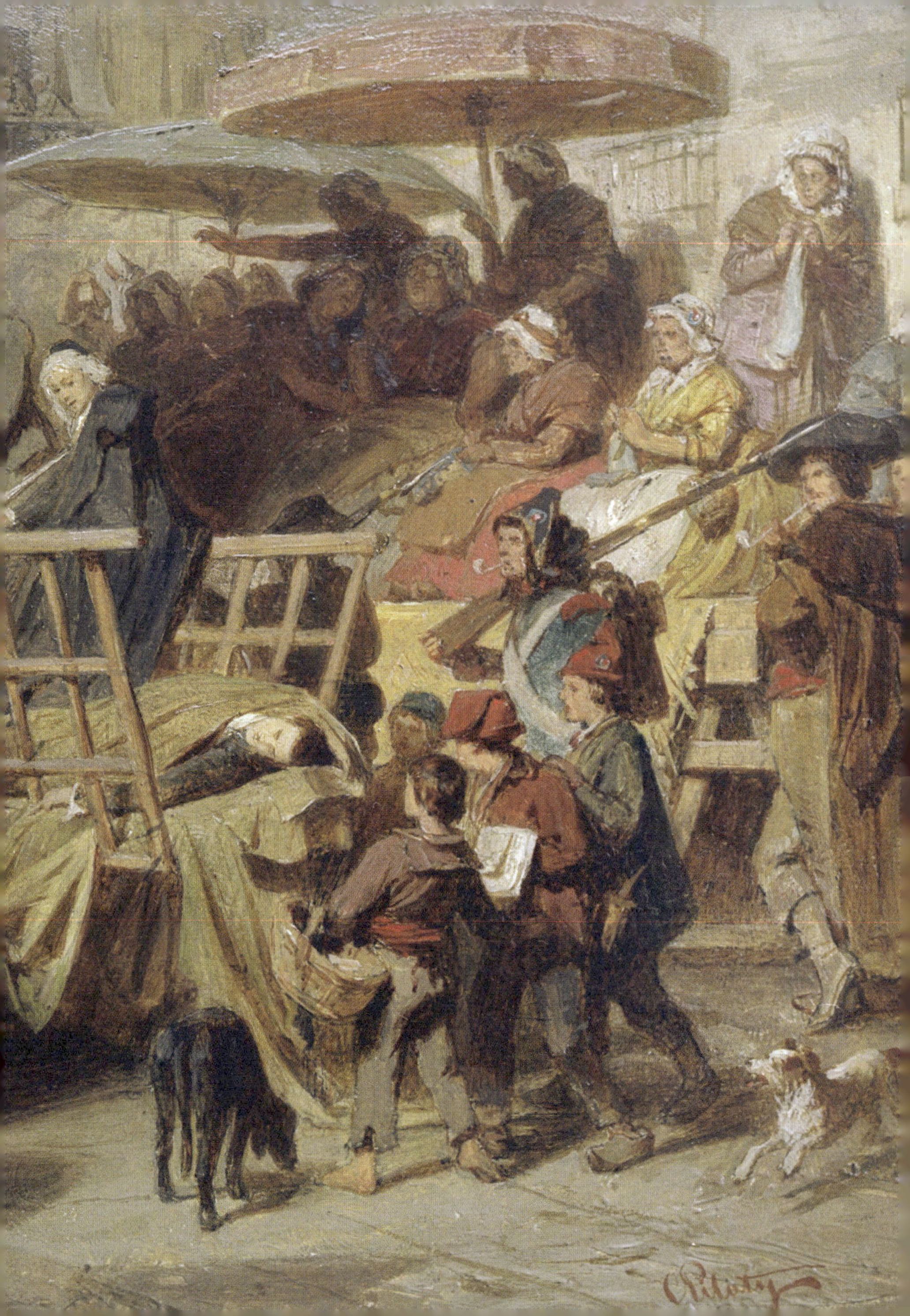

# V.

The lust for vengeance is endemic

Karl Theodor von Piloty, *The Last Moments of the Girondists*, 1880. Towards the back of the painting the *tricoteuse* enjoy the entertainment of the guillotine with their knitting in hand.

The *tricoteuse* at the guillotine

In order to get well, we should depress ourselves further. The French Revolution lasted ten years, from 5th May 1789 until 9th November 1799. In this period of chaos and savagery, one year stands out as especially heinous: the Reign of Terror of 1793-1794, when the guillotine worked nonstop in the Place de la Révolution (now the Place de la Concorde). Carts arrived by the half-hour from the prisons of France, bearing suspected counter-revolutionaries, aristocrats, parliamentarians, moderates, peacemakers and other enemies of so-called friendship and justice. They were hauled onto a wooden platform, forced to apologise to the crowd and murdered, before their severed heads were placed on spikes and lined up for exhibition along the bridges of Paris.

At the foot the guillotine, where one could get the best view and there was room for chairs, would be a raucous group of women from the poorest districts of Paris, the so-called *tricoteuse*, or 'knitters'. They would come at dawn with snacks and drinks and spend the day watching one unfortunate after another lose their head, while they roared with laughter, chatted, exchanged notes on the weather – and did some knitting.

It is the contrast between the unhurried, domestic work of knitting and the simultaneous extinction of life that is hard to swallow. We may wonder at how hearts could become so deformed, but the sheer number of knitting onlookers tell us that we are not dealing with isolated cases of pathology. This isn't about one or two sick minds afforded an unusual chance to exhibit their ailments during an unprecedented national crisis; this is who we are.

The tricoteuse point to a dreadful truth about the suffering of others: that we enjoy it. We are relieved by it; it makes our day. We need others to fail, we hope ardently that they might and it will be an ecstatic moment when they do. We will show up with a gang and point and laugh, we will remark on your clothing and your hairstyle as you march up the steps, we won't care a jot that you were once a child and that you have goodness still in your soul, we will latch on to every reason to believe in your wickedness. We'll trust in the rumours, we won't scrutinise the allegations and you won't appear human to us any more. Our hearts will stay cold as your neck is placed on the block and a razor-sharp blade ruptures your arteries.

By what mysterious process do humans become like this? What happens to a newborn to turn them, over the years, into a *tricoteur*? If only the journey were more arduous or uncommon. All that seems to be required to fill up the mind with reserves of vengeance and fury is a steady drip-feed of humiliation of the kind that every life is likely to provide. We have all been made sufficiently unhappy so as to gain extraordinary respite and satisfaction from the downfalls of others.

Public executions are rare, but the tricoteuse are always with us. They are in the office, watching as we collect our belongings and are led out of the building; they are at the party, listening with feigned innocence as someone recounts the story of a divorce; they try to suppress a smile at the announcement of our disgrace; and, of course, they are at their keyboards as the comments roll in declaiming someone as a failure.

We cannot stop them, unless we were to succeed in eradicating every vestige of unhappiness in every life. Until then, not only will we have to suffer, but we will have to know that this suffering will bring immense joy to others. Our only protection is pessimism towards the many, and extreme love towards the few rare, unsullied beings who remain unhurt enough that they will cry when it's our time to step up to the scaffold.

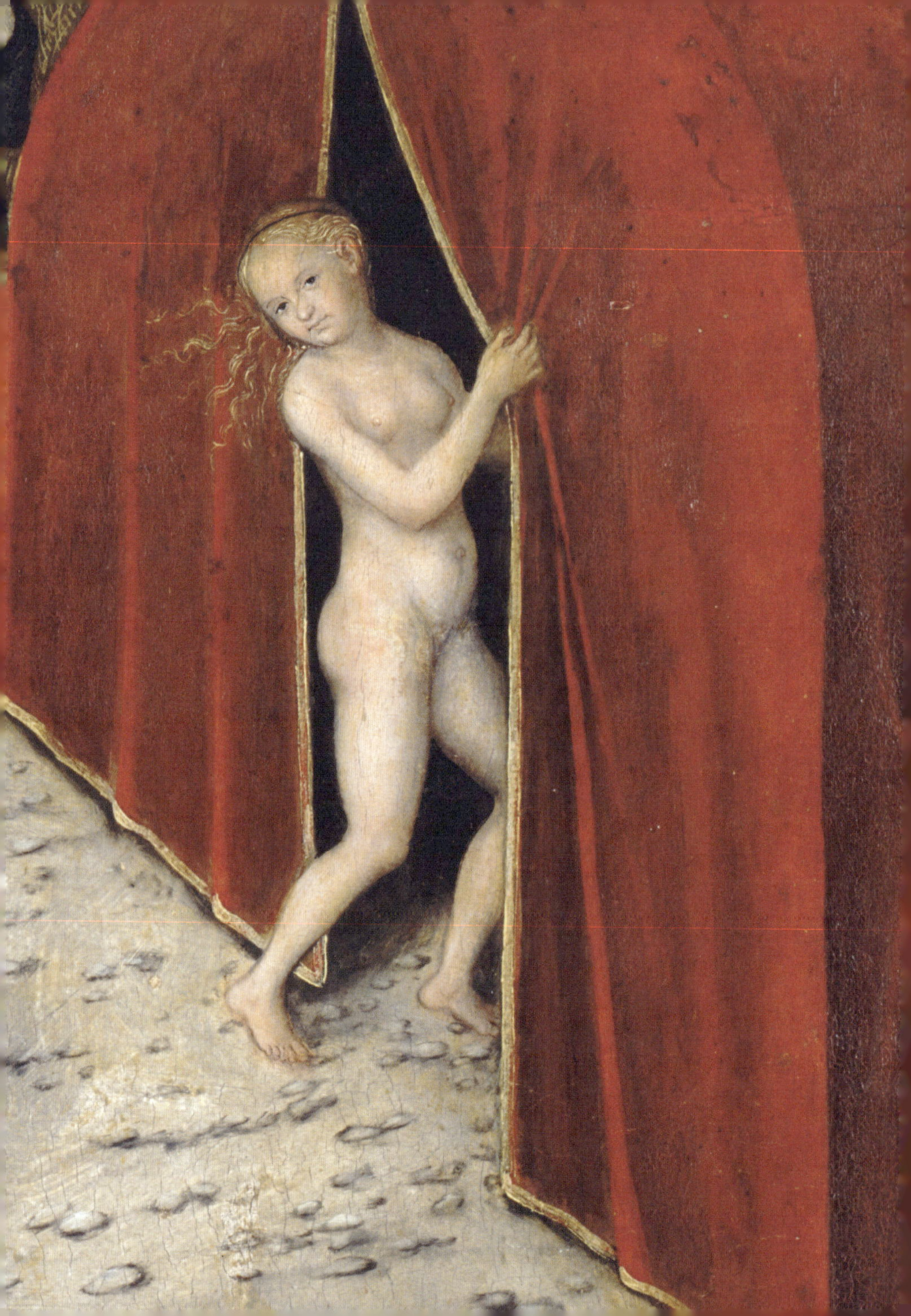

VI.

We regret so much

Lucas Cranach the Elder, *The Fountain of Youth*, 1546 (detail).
A nubile and athletic bather emerges from the Fountain of Youth –
a reminder of time and regret.

The Fountain of Youth

On the left-hand side of the painting, the old arrive from across the land by horse, cart and wheelbarrow. One especially pitiful character staggers in on someone's back. By the water's edge, exhausted, they strip off their rags and heavy cloaks and, under the gaze of a doctor, clamber gingerly into the pool. Their skin is grey and sallow, their limbs heavy and pockmarked – but within a few steps, the magical properties of the Fountain of Youth start to work their effects. Suppleness returns, stomachs become firm again, cheeks fill out, necks return to their original tautness. By the time they reach the other end of the pool, the bathers have become nubile and athletic, they giggle and saunter, they can run without pain and their hair is luxuriant and their eyes bright; all the intervening decades have been wiped away and they start their adult lives once more. A group of handsome knights wait to give them new clothes and direct them to an elegant, curtained-off changing room, before inviting them on to a banquet and a dance.

By the time Lucas Cranach the Elder finished his depiction in 1546, the idea of a Fountain of Youth had been a well-established trope of European art and literature for two centuries. Many a medieval fable ended with an elderly couple, under the guidance of a kindly wizard, arriving at a

Lucas Cranach the Elder, *The Fountain of Youth*, 1546

fountain or pool bubbling with magical warm waters that would catapult them back to their adolescence in moments.

Ostensibly, the legend captures our longing to recover physical grace, but its hold on our imaginations runs deeper. It isn't just our bodies we miss; it's our potential. There is so much that we failed to notice and to do, so many opportunities we squandered, so many mistakes we could have avoided. There are people we should never have loved and others we should have dared to declare ourselves to; there are professional opportunities we should have pushed harder to secure and traps and lures we should have resisted. We should not have been so cowardly and so conventional. We should have been clearer about what we wanted and we should have stopped expecting that someone would rescue us from our inactivity and vagueness. We should have taken so much more care with certain relationships and we shouldn't have been so vain and impressed by public opinion. We should have been modest, resolute, dignified, serious and kind – the way we always wanted to be. We have betrayed ourselves.

We can never bathe in Cranach's healing waters, but we can take a little solace in the knowledge that our grief is not ours alone. All of us are obsessed with the wish to go back and warn our younger selves of the dangers – all of us are victims of an inherently excruciating existence that forces us to rush forward blindly, only ever understanding things when it is already much too late.

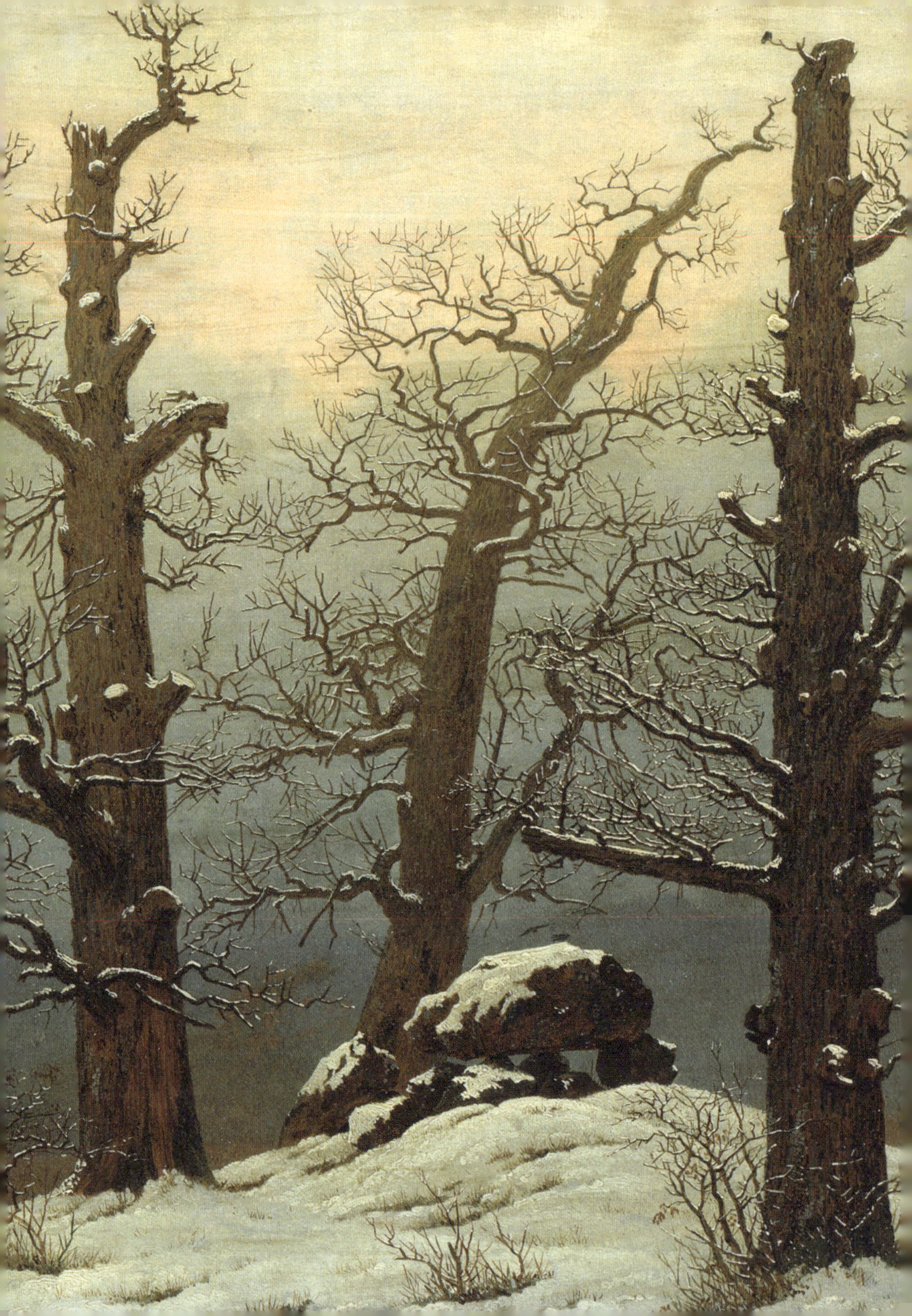

VII.

The advantages of sadness

Caspar David Friedrich, *Dolmen in the Snow*, 1807 (detail).
The sadness of a winter landscape, providing comfort to the melancholic.

Bitterness vs melancholy

We have started by framing a selection of dark arguments as 'reasons to be hopeful'. There are different ways of dealing with the negative aspects of life, some a lot more helpful than others. We might draw a distinction between two fundamental ways of relating to misfortune: *bitterness* on the one hand and *melancholy* on the other.

Both the bitter and the melancholy person are upset, and both may weep, but from here there are major differences. The bitter person believes that the terrible things that have happened to them are an aberration. They were not part of the plan. There should have been justice, the bitter person insists, because the world is a fundamentally just place – it is simply one that has dealt them, and only them, a set of unwarranted cards. They are consumed by resentment and will examine their wounds until the day they die.

Like the bitter person, the *melancholy* person has been punished – but they never take the additional step of assuming that their suffering is an exception. Even if their neighbours don't seem to be going through anything like what they themselves have been allotted, they assume that these people will have their own momentous challenges going on behind the scenes. The melancholy don't assume that life is easy for anyone, even the so-called privileged; they are not deceived by outward smiles or access to material luxuries. At the same time, they do not for an instant maintain that there is justice behind suffering. They understand that punishments are handed out without close reference to anyone's character. There is no due process behind disease or injury: the world isn't some sort of law court or exam board. They know that there is little merit behind success or failure; most of the terrible things that occur do so entirely randomly, as a result of the demented swerves of the juggernaut of fate.

These two philosophies explain the different outlooks of the bitter and the melancholy. The bitter person is restless, their agitation constant and their fury never exhausts itself. Meanwhile, the melancholy person is serene. They quickly take on board the nightmares that have befallen them, but they had half-expected them all along. They are capable of smiling, and even laughing, in a sad way. They don't incline to anger, because there is no one to be angry with; they never signed a contract for happiness that has been reneged.

When it comes to art, the melancholy gain comfort from engaging with pessimistic creators. These artists don't zero in on specific tragedies, labelling them as injustices they want to campaign against. They take it for granted that life will always be a painful business. 'Man's greatness comes from knowing he is wretched,' observed Blaise Pascal. 'Anyone who does not see the vanity of the world is very vain himself.' There is a comparable wisdom in Arthur Schopenhauer, who said of life: 'It is bad today and every day it will get worse until the worst of all happens.' And, no less acutely: 'Human existence must be a kind of error.' The final word, however, should belong to the greatest of all melancholy thinkers, the Stoic philosopher Seneca: 'What need is there to weep over parts of life? The whole of it calls for tears.'

To spend time with pessimistic works isn't dispiriting; rather it tends to cheer us up, precisely because what brings us down is a sense that we might be alone in our misery. The dark thinkers provide a perspective from which our own travails burden us less. We gladly join in shared currents of torment. We smile from relief.

Equal relief is to be found by looking through the eyes of melancholy painters. They too have no need to tell us exactly what has gone wrong in their own lives. The great 19th-century German painter Caspar David Friedrich need only show us some trees in winter or a meadow after a rain shower and we understand. We know that this

Caspar David Friedrich, *The Large Enclosure*

(also known as *The Great Preserve*) in Dresden, 1831–1832

painter inhabits the same world as we do, that he has had similar experiences of loss and regret and sadness in his hinterland.

Friedrich depicts particular parts of northern Germany, but he simultaneously gives shape to corners of our own souls. We are cheered because, although the works are sober in the extreme, they give us a language with which to externalise and render more comprehensible a sadness that lies heavily on our own hearts.

There is no reason for bitterness: we were never promised an easy ride. Indeed, we should always have been alive to the basic obscenity of life. It is understandable if we might want to give up and surrender to rage, but it is truer still to keep going, to know every single last dark fact and be aware of every miserable detail and yet still maintain a steady, sad gaze out onto the sombre landscape – all the while keeping a small, quiet eye out for dawn.

2.

Reasons of Detachment

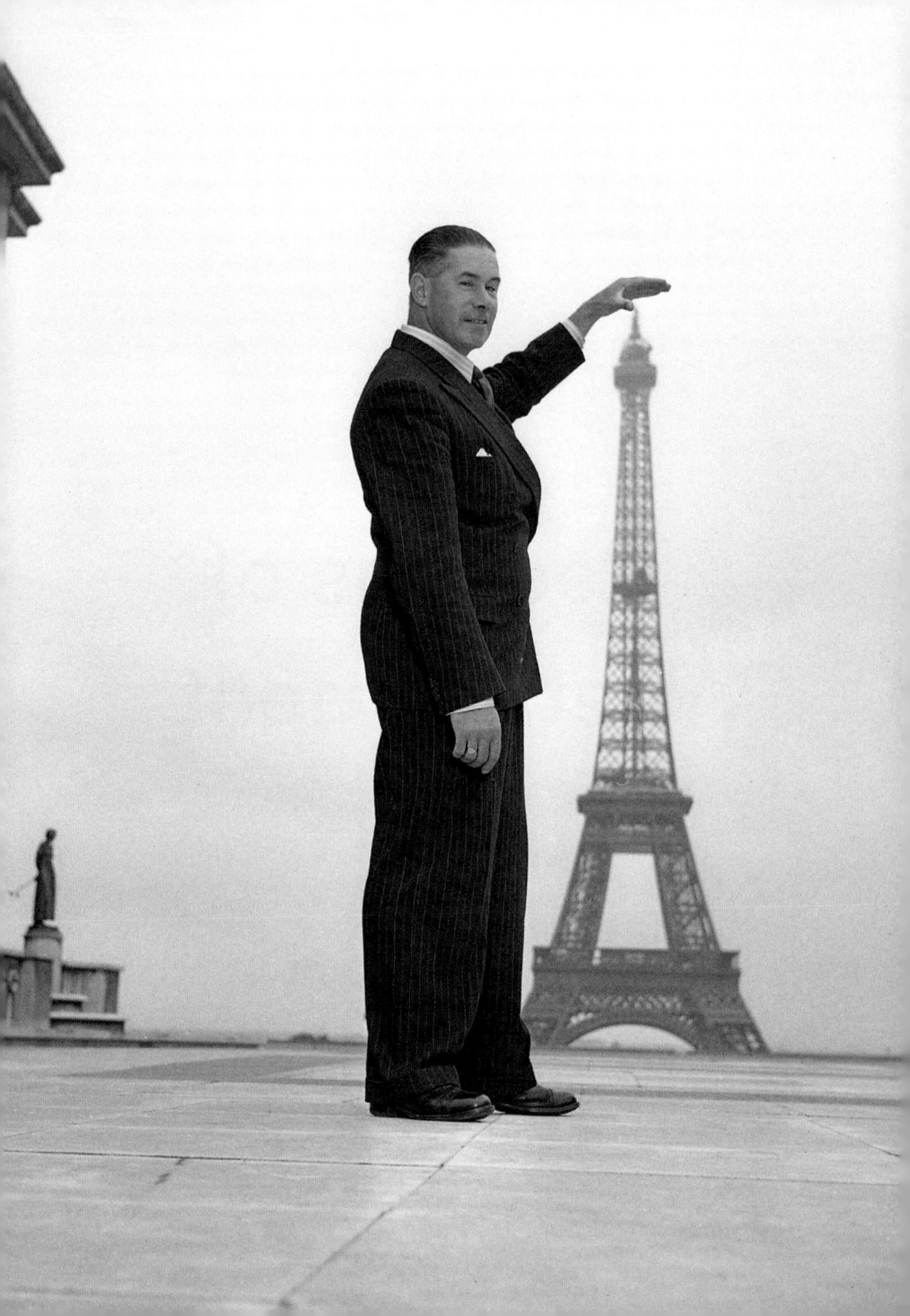

I.

We need perspective

The Eiffel Tower, Paris, 1956. The problem is that we haven't yet developed similar techniques for addressing the more urgent and intimate problem of emotional perspective.

The giant and the Eiffel Tower

The Eiffel Tower is gigantic: 324 metres to the tip of the mast, enough to render even the tallest person minute by comparison. But, depending on where we happen to be standing, the proportions may be wildly reversed. The immensely sturdy tower can appear as fragile and diminutive as a toy, and a person can look like a monster.

The freakish tricks of perspective that can be generated in a photograph reveal something powerful about how our brains work: we are instinctively prone to exaggerate the scale of whatever happens to be close to us. The place that this really causes us problems isn't our vision, but an area where the issue is much harder to detect: our emotional lives.

A pain, fear, worry or regret that's in our minds right now has the habit of occupying the whole of our attention and denying us every opportunity for rest or hope. Things that might offer reassurance recede and feel insubstantial. If we could take a photograph of our inner state, our distress would be like a threatening giant, while the elements that give stability and worth to our lives (a good friendship, a skill, a long history of dealing with challenges) would disappear into nothingness.

From Hans Vredeman de Vries, *Perspective*, 1604

With vision, it took humanity a long time to understand and to master the techniques of correct perspective. In the early 15th century, the Italian architect and sculptor Filippo Brunelleschi devised specific exercises to help improve his skills in this area. Over time, he and many others acquired a remarkable facility in the new science of visual perspective. By the 1600s, clear and simple manuals were widely available that allowed anyone who wished to become, quite easily, adept at what had once seemed an almost impossibly difficult task.

The problem is that we haven't yet developed similar techniques for addressing the more urgent and intimate problem of emotional perspective.

The ideal manual for developing such a skill might point to four important exercises. The first is simply to admit to oneself that the problem exists; to acknowledge that our instincts about how big an emotional issue is can be very easily mistaken. It's a surprisingly hard step to take, because in our worried moments it rarely feels like we have got anything out of proportion; we insist that the problem is exactly as ghastly as it seems. This is where we need to marshal our memories. We all know that in the past we've exaggerated the severity of problems: we've flown into a huge, despairing rage or sunk into a deep sulk over things that, in retrospect, really weren't all that significant. We should draw on such recollections to calm us down when it seems – this time for sure – to be the end of the world. Even if we can't be sure exactly *why* it isn't actually the end of the world, past experience will point us to an overall sense that it most likely won't be. We can learn to distrust the certainties that accompany our own panic.

A second exercise involves encouraging ourselves to adopt a much wider field of imaginative vision. As a point of reference, contemplate for a moment the Great Comet of 1577, which blazed a dazzling trail across the night sky from October of that year to the end of January 1578, and was observed around the world, from Peru to China. And then it disappeared.

It seemed to many at the time that the comet heralded the destruction of the planet or marked the opening of a wonderful new epoch of world history, but really it meant nothing of the kind. We know now that it was just an icy lump of rock on an eccentric path across the universe that brought it, briefly, close to Earth. It is now somewhere beyond the orbit of Neptune, heading into the lonely wastes on the fringes of the solar system; it is not expected ever to return. Our strong emotions are like the comet:

Unknown artist, the Great Comet of 1577,

Turkish miniature, Nusrat-Namah, 1584

flaring briefly and seeming to mean so much. But on the vast scale of the cosmos, they are the tiniest specks and briefest moments. They don't have the tremendous import we think they do and, before long, they will vanish.

The third exercise to teach emotional perception is to remind ourselves that a life – from our start as a baby to old age – is a very long and very complicated process.

What seems overwhelming to us now will count for little in retrospect. Our tens of thousands of days will blend and be forgotten. To contemplate an image of the very old and the very young side by side is to be reminded that the current moment is a tiny sliver of our whole existence. We will have millions of disappointments, worries and satisfactions. What is in our mind at this moment is far from determining the totality of who we are.

Finally, as a last step towards recognising the true scale of our woes, we should focus our thoughts on the sufferings of others. What we are going through right now is surely bad – but it's unlikely, for example, to equal the drama of an average day in an accident and emergency ward.

We could, and perhaps one day will, be on a hospital trolley surrounded by frantic medical professionals cutting away the bloody fragments of our clothing, inserting tubes into our nostrils and anxiously checking our wildly fluctuating heart rate. Our current problem seems utterly intense to us because it's in our minds and occupies the front row of our consciousness, but we can recognise that other people have worse situations to live with. This doesn't mean that we don't deserve compassion, just that we are not as fragile as we feel we might be.

Emotional perspective doesn't pretend that our troubles aren't real. It's not trying to brush them aside; rather it's seeking a more important and wiser insight: an accurate assessment of their scale. To be ignominiously fired from a job, for instance, is obviously hugely distressing, but the instinct may nonetheless be to exaggerate this event beyond its actual dimensions.

We feel that this will be the end of our career, that it means our entire life has been ruined or that we'll never get over the humiliation. In these moments, we need to remind ourselves that this too will pass, that the comet of tears will one day leave our firmament and that, however unlikely the thought might seem, calmer days will return.

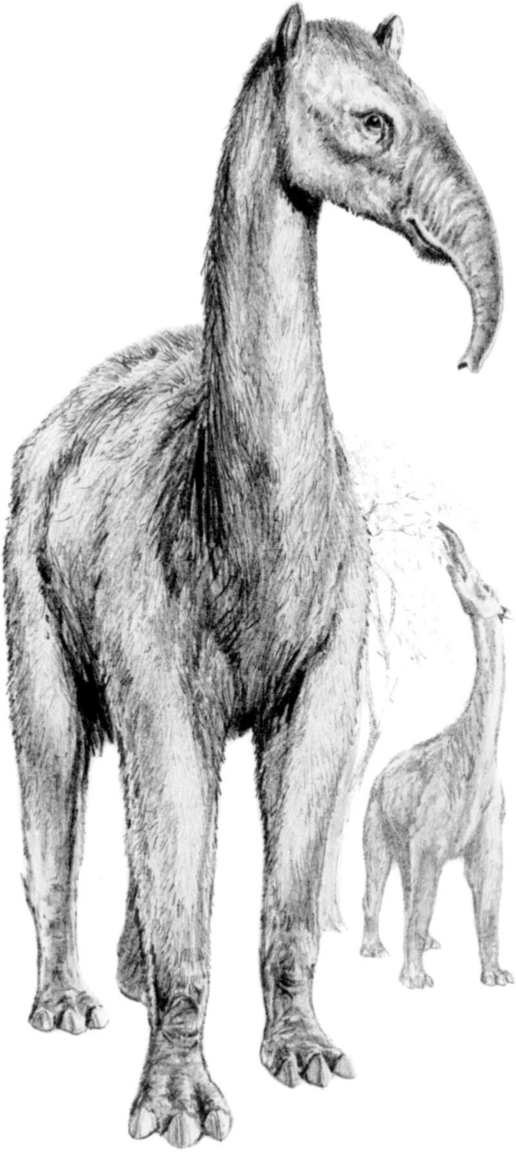

II.

The ultimate fate of humanity is not our business

Macrauchenia. This extinct prehistoric mammal, which lived 7 million to 20,000 years ago, is a reminder that a great many things are not in our power.

The end of the macrauchenia

Given the scale of the perils that face humanity, it is hardly surprising if serenity and peace of mind are hard to come by. Reasons to panic are daily brought before our eyes by the ever inquisitive and always alarming modern media: there are wildfires raging across South America and Australia; currency manipulation is rife; people smugglers are working with impunity in Eastern Europe; bureaucracy is stifling innovation across the prosperous world; the air in large cities is more polluted than ever; soon there will be no more snow leopards, orangutans or leatherback sea turtles; and there's a new kind of gigantic pink seaweed threatening the health of the southern oceans. It's a wonder we ever sleep.

At moments of particular alarm, we would do well to turn our thoughts to the macrauchenia. For millions of years, this delightful, camel-sized animal flourished across what we now call South America, being found in its largest numbers in northern Argentina. It was a placid herbivore, with an endearingly droopy nose, a soft, fleecy coat and warm, contemplative eyes, which lived in small family groups, browsing inoffensively on the leaves of the jacaranda tree and in the evenings trooping down to the many shallow lakes of the region to bathe.

Though the macrauchenia had a very good run, it sadly didn't make it in the end. It flourished during the Palaeogene, a geologic era that spanned 43 million years, from the end of the Cretaceous period 66 million years ago to the beginning of the Neogene period. But then its fortunes ran out. The species was decimated by newer, aggressive creatures that came down from North America during the Great American Biotic Interchange, after the establishment of the Central American land bridge. The last macrauchenia is estimated to have died (probably in the jaws of some kind of prairie dog) about 10,000 years before the arrival of stooped early humans at the end of the Pleistocene period. It was Charles Darwin who, on a short stopover near Puerto San Julián in Patagonia in 1838, uncovered the first macrauchenia skeleton and gave the animal its name.

The macrauchenia would have been charming to know and deeply helpful to the farmers of South America, but their loss was not unusual. In fact, 99.9 per cent of all organisms that have ever existed have been wiped out across the five mass extinctions of history. Five times over the last 500 million years, life has more or less had to start again from scratch. It is hugely unlikely that the species we are currently worried about, such as the Bornean elephant or the Ganges river dolphin, will make it in the long term.

Our own fate necessarily hangs in the balance as well. It would take a resolute optimist to venture that we will not, in time, follow the example of most of our forebears, including the narrow-nosed rhinoceros, the flat-headed peccary and the dwarf hippo. This might seem like an entirely tragic thought, but it has a relieving aspect as well. It is common that we feel overburdened by a momentous sense of responsibility for what is to come. We worry about peace conferences, the paths of gas pipelines, the vagaries of unemployment insurance and the levels of nitrogen in the soil. These are fine ways to mop up anxiety, but in the grander scheme we might as well be weeping over the long-distant demise of a friendly South American odd-toed ungulate.

The news constantly provides us with a ringside seat for the most compelling and horrendous issues of our times, which feed both our outrage and our sense that there must be something we can do to try to prevent disaster. But in the process, we forget the radical limits on our powers to intervene effectively in pretty much any of the dilemmas that bedevil our species. It is our particular fate to know more than we ever have done about the troubles of our fellow humans and yet to remain almost wholly ineffective at finding solutions – not because we are uncreative or lethargic, but because we have been granted, at best, a teaspoon with which to drain an ocean. Our planet is shaped by gigantic forces – financial, political, biological, extraterrestrial – against which our individual wills are doomed to be substantially powerless. We have about as much chance of altering the dynamics behind our catastrophes as we have of shifting the orbital patterns of the moons of Jupiter.

There may be a few steps we can take to dampen our crises, but they will tend to be close to home and to concern the welfare of only a handful of people. We should not be harsh or unjust towards ourselves. We didn't personally create the world and we are not individually responsible for its fate.

As we contemplate the extinct macrauchenia, we are seeing an image of our own small innocence and admitting a liberating truth: a great many things are not in our power to control and we needn't feel in charge of them. A few of the more nervous, fretful macrauchenia might once have worried about the survival of their race as evening fell and giant anteaters rustled in the bushes, but the truly wise and contented ones would have loved their families, planned the evening meal for the little ones and refrained from fretting too much about what was to come over the coming million years.

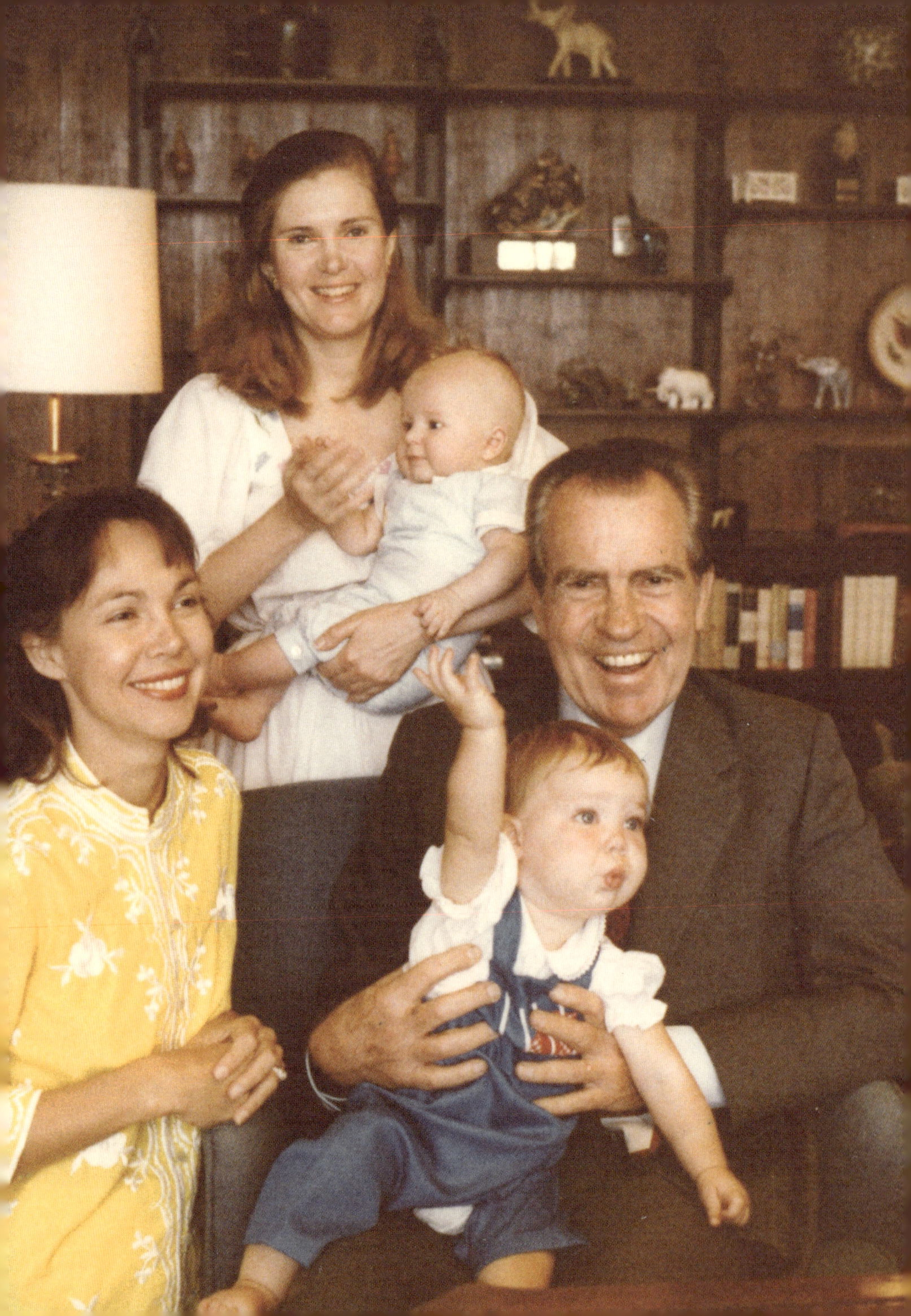

III.

If it all collapsed, we'd be fine, eventually

President Nixon, displaying the possibilities of recovery, spends time with his daughters and grandchildren.

A day with Grandfather

It's been a lovely day with Grandfather; Aunt Julie and Uncle David came by with their children, Jenny, Melanie and Alex; little Christopher is nearly 4.

It's all pleasantly normal and average, except that the grandfather is Richard Nixon, a man who once had the nuclear codes in his office, who engineered the end of the Vietnam War – and who, in 1974, would have been put on trial for obstruction of justice and abuse of power and sent to prison if he hadn't received a pardon from his successor as president of the United States, Gerald Ford.

We'll never face the level of condemnation that Richard Nixon did; no disgrace of ours can ever match his. And yet, after years of soul-searching – and with the sheer passage of time – he was able to pull together a worthwhile existence. Eventually, it became possible for him once more to take pleasure in digging the garden, in spending the afternoon with his family and in catching up with old acquaintances.

For many people, of course, Nixon was simply an appalling man, utterly undeserving of sympathy. We might be tempted to think of him in a different light, however, when we too have badly messed up and earned the contempt of others. Then Nixon becomes not just a famously bad person, but a version of our own flawed selves.

Nixon's failings were played out on the largest scale. Our own disasters may be more modest and local, but we too have often been the shamefully guilty party.

What Nixon is sending us, via an ordinary family snap, is a message about the possibilities of recovery. He wasn't an adept apologist, he didn't make a grand return, he never shook off the widespread conviction that he was a devious character. But he was able to adjust and still find genuine sources of goodness and contentment in his existence. What makes his example all the more touching is that he did this without being in any way uniquely skilled at redemption. He was still a flawed, awkward man – he wasn't coming to the task of recovery with better chances than we have. In our own dark moments, this image speaks to us of our future: modest and ordinary, but genuinely OK – a state that in troubled times seems almost more than we can dare to hope for.

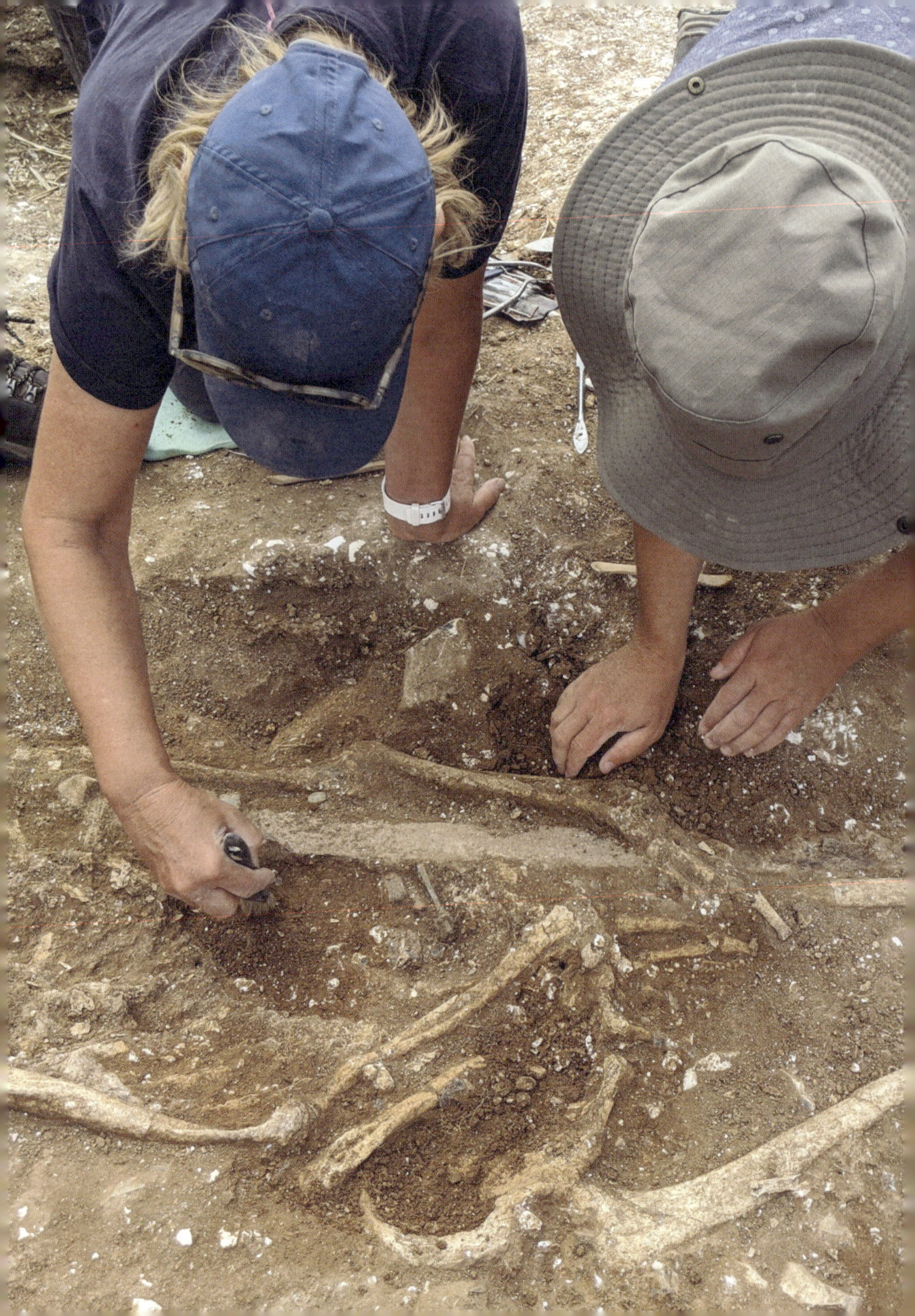

IV.

The equality of eternity

Archaeologists excavating the site of a long-dead Anglo Saxon king known as the 'Marlow Warlord', Berkshire, UK. The distinctions and achievements that seem to matter so much in life will eventually lose their meaning.

The bones of the chief

In life, he was a great chieftain. After the withdrawal of the Roman army from Britain, he and his clan carved out a kingdom for themselves in the area that today lies just west of London. He led his people on daring raids on villages across the river; they sang his praises as they caroused around the campfire at night. He was a tall man for the time, evidently a ferocious fighter. He was famous and feared in all the surrounding lands.

When he died, they buried him with all possible honour on a small hill overlooking a bend of the River Thames: the strategic centre of their territory. Even in death, he would be the one to guide and protect them. They laid him out in his grave with his great sword and his treasured glass beaker – a prestigious rarity – beside him. The women wailed for days; the men lit funeral bonfires. And then time passed. His kingdom was conquered, his Anglo-Saxon people became the serfs to the new invading masters, the Normans. Quiet tenant farmers grazed their sheep on the lands he had won in battle. Eventually a railway line was constructed nearby, suburban villas sprang up and, on tranquil evenings, retired solicitors and affable bank clerks and their wives would walk their dogs on the springy turf above his grave.

A ferocious Anglo-Saxon military chief, famous and feared in life,

forgotten in death.

The Winter Hill Golf Club laid out its fairways and sand bunkers where he had once mustered his loyal troops, and a branch of a major supermarket chain opened within sight of his resting place. On windy days families would come over to fly kites, not realising that they were standing just a few feet above the fragments of his skull.

And then, in 2018, a couple of local amateur archaeologists, armed with a metal detector, decided to explore the field. Alerted by the beeping of their machine, they began, very carefully, to remove the topsoil. His fine sword was half eaten away by rust, its beautiful leather scabbard all but disintegrated; worms and beetles had consumed his flesh, most of his bones had crumbled and the roots of a gorse bush had grown through his ribcage.

There's a shocking, poignant contrast between what he once was and what became of him. His status, possessions and strength were entirely forgotten. The pagan gods he worshipped were replaced first by Christianity and then by an indifferent atheism. But this is not a fate peculiar to him. With time it will happen to us all. All the great people of today will eventually be forgotten; their graves will be lost, the entire culture that gave them their prominence and rich rewards will disappear and archaeologists will one day strive to decipher their identities.

It's an oddly comforting thought: the distinctions and achievements that seem to matter so much in life will eventually lose their meaning. An ultimate equality of neglect will unite everyone. It won't matter who was the chief and who the pauper. Even better, we don't have to wait centuries for this sense of equality to take hold – we can summon the inevitable future into our imaginations right now. The youthful billionaire, the celebrity athlete, the handsome entrepreneur, the glamorous socialite – all will be returned to unity with us. As we look at their faces in a magazine or watch them on our screens, it is as if we can already see the future in which they will, like us, be crumpled, anonymous bones in a forgotten patch of our gloriously indifferent earth.

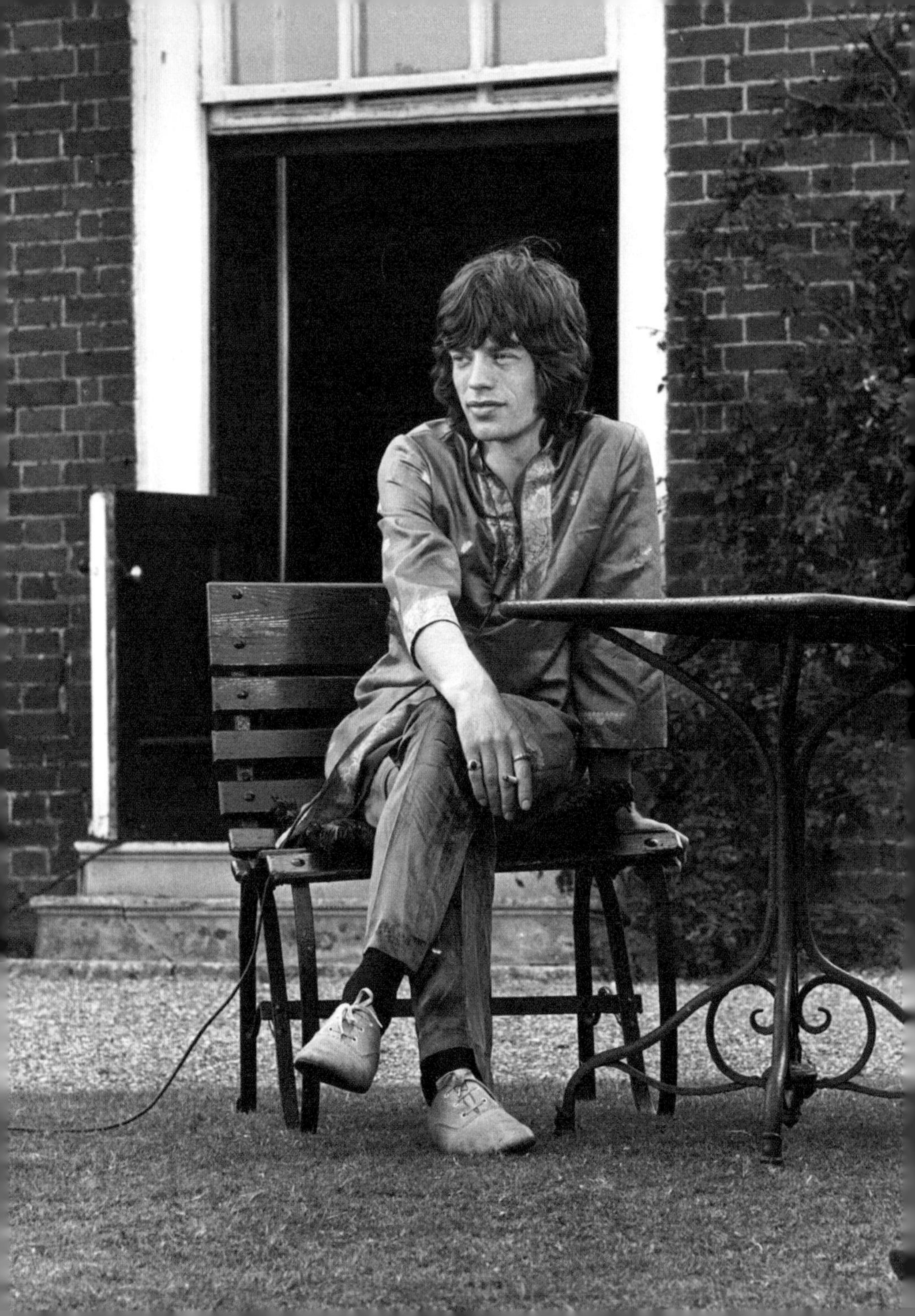

v.

Live in voluntary exile

Mick Jagger, at the height of his fame and cultural influence, filming *World in Action*, 31st July 1967

Mick Jagger and the Jesuit priest

One of the great moments of television history occurred in July 1967. Mick Jagger – then at the height of his fame and cultural influence – was helicoptered into the gardens of a large country house in the south-east of England to discuss his views on modern life with a group of distinguished establishment figures. The producers had picked these people for one provocative reason above any other: they knew nothing about Jagger or his music.

One of the desperately out-of-touch interlocutors was a Jesuit priest and former master of an Oxford College, Thomas Corbishley, S.J. He immediately admitted that not only did he know nothing about the Rolling Stones, he'd never heard a single song by any modern band. He was nevertheless extremely interested in Mick Jagger and he probed the star in a patient and kindly way to reveal more about his positive beliefs, rather than what he was against.

To the many millions of people who watched the show, Corbishley must have seemed comedically out of touch – a ridiculous antiquarian relic, cut off from the freedom, authenticity and liberation of modernity. But in his own way, he can be seen as the truly heroic and independent

Mick Jagger discussing his attitudes towards society with four leaders of the establishment, one of whom, the Jesuit priest Thomas Corbishley (centre, in clerical collar) – a truly heroic and independent figure – knew nothing of the Rolling Stones or Jagger.

figure of the meeting, with much to teach his own times and our own. He had opted, against massive societal pressure, not to follow the herd, but instead to pursue issues that were dear to him. Whatever the widespread enthusiasm for 'Sympathy for the Devil' and 'Honky Tonk Women', Corbishley's interests lay elsewhere: he had translated the *Spiritual Exercises of St Ignatius of Loyola*, written commentaries on St Augustine, published a biography of the Jesuit priest Pierre Teilhard de Chardin and, in a number of books, explored what it meant to be a Catholic in the wake of the Second Vatican Council.

The priest was pursuing what one might term a 'strategy of voluntary exile' from the current preoccupations of his society. He didn't feel any need to keep up with the flotsam and jetsam of contemporary culture; he felt closer to what was happening in Paris in 1254, when Thomas Aquinas wrote *On Being and Essence* in defence of the Dominican community, than what was unfolding in Mary Quant's shop on the King's Road in London in October 1965 (the first batch of miniskirts had just been launched). Corbishley was content to be thought ridiculous because he had his own well-defined concept of seriousness to hand.

We may not quite realise the extent to which we have mortgaged our inner lives to the received ideas that are, actually, grievously alien to our true selves. We start to be free when we can dare to become wilfully ignorant – when we no longer have to know the names of certain musicians that everyone esteems, when we don't feel compelled to read particular books that have won prizes, when we are left cold by holiday destinations, clothes, foods, exercise regimes, political scandals and ideas that are dominant, when we can stay home rather than attend parties with people we dislike and when we can hear of a celebrity and genuinely wonder who they might be. It is hard enough to have to exist in any given era; we don't in addition have to mould our souls in its image.

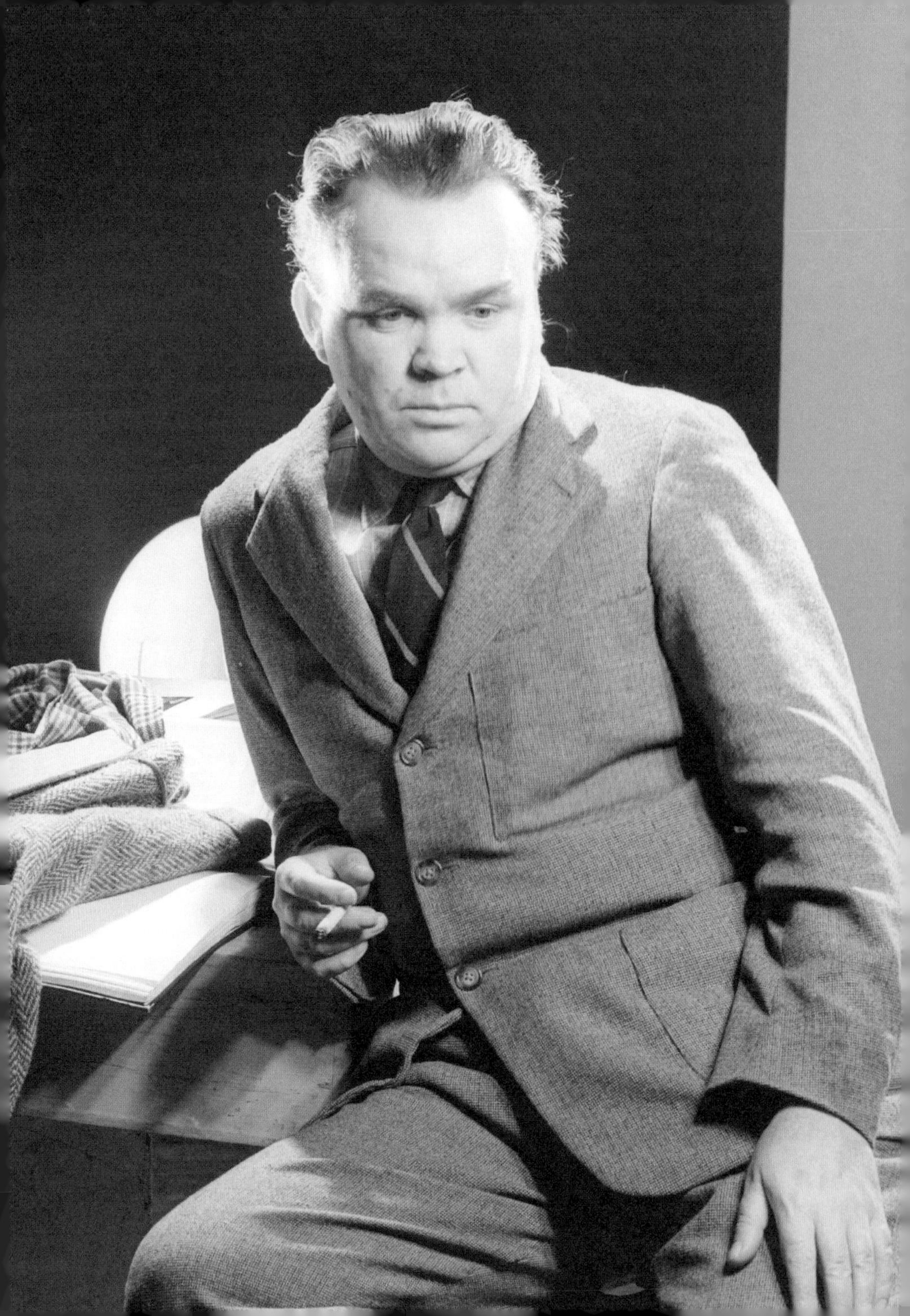

VI.

We have blessedly poor memories

A portrait of Cyril Connolly by schoolmate Cecil Beaton, 1942.
Our memory serves us well in forgetting those moments of misery from our school years that so deeply upset us at the time.

Cyril Connolly's exercise book

We often complain that we have bad memories. We forget our house keys, the names of certain acquaintances and vital items from the shopping list. But what might count as a rank nuisance on a practical level turns out to be an unparalleled blessing on an emotional one. We are rescued from many of our sorrows not by active solutions or nifty work of the intellect, but by our reliable tendencies to forget. Our minds are so constituted that the gravest incidents eventually slip from our grasp. We lose sight not only of the beautiful and kind things that have occurred – the Bay of Naples at dawn, the taste of figs in autumn and the first night spent in the company of a lover – but also, more usefully, the catalogue of horrors that we were once certain we would never be able to surmount. However hysterically sad we may feel, we can rely on the knowledge that we will soon forget what we are crying about.

When in his 50s, the great English literary critic and essayist Cyril Connolly discovered a Latin grammar textbook that he had had at around the age of 10, when he had attended a fashionable preparatory school in Eastbourne, St Cyprian's. On the flyleaf of the book, he had written in his most careful script, 'Never [underlined three times] forget how unhappy you were today, February 11th, 1913.' Now, many decades later, he hadn't the faintest recollection of what had so deeply upset him on that distant day, even though it must have seemed as if it would burn forever in his thoughts, sending echoes of misery across the entirety of his existence.

Our habit of forgetting might feel like a betrayal. A part of us wants to remain eternally loyal to the sufferings that consume our thoughts and to which our identities can feel indelibly bound. But our minds are efficient, unsentimental places that need to clear space for novel experiences, so eventually even our worst recollections become hazy and neutered. We might realise that years have gone by without having given a single thought to a mistake that we had once imagined would darken our lives in perpetuity.

We may lament our far-from-perfect memories, but we should be grateful for them. If we had a recollection of every occasion when someone had been unkind to us, of every slight that had come our way, every mistake we had committed and every hope that had been frustrated, life would swiftly grow untenable. Fortunately, we have been endowed with a special incapacity. The slate is always, gradually being wiped clean, ensuring that we end up ignorant of what once left us certain that we should end our lives by nightfall.

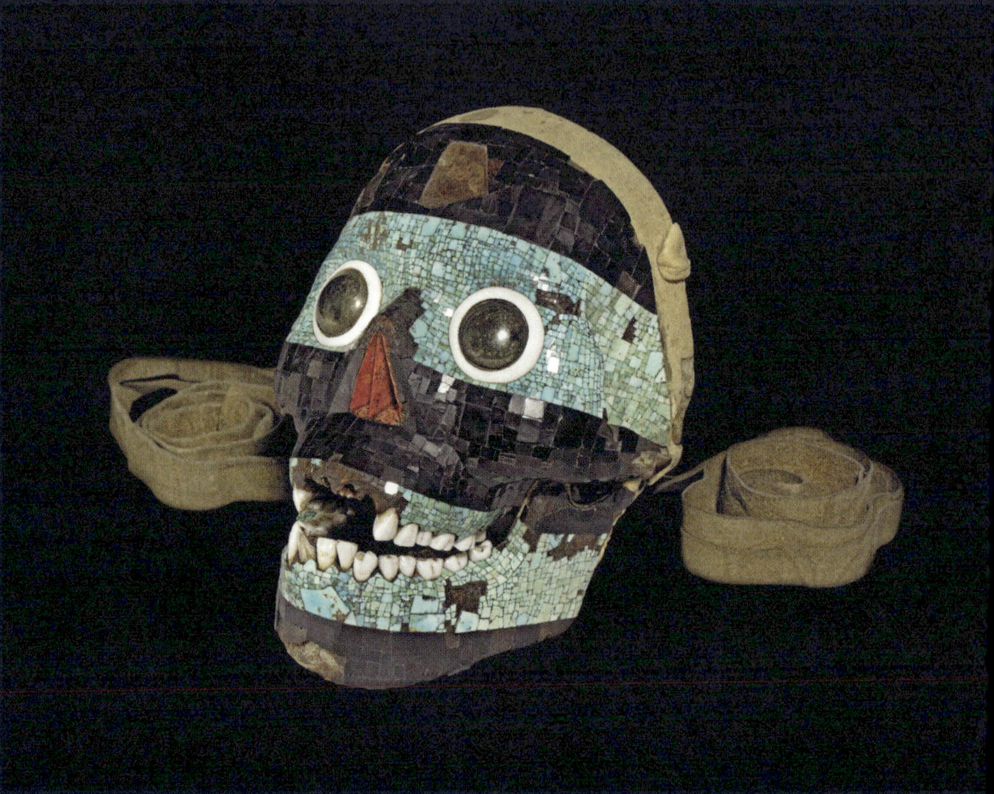

VII.

Much of what others believe is nonsense

Turquoise mosaic skull representing Tezcatlipoca, c. 1400–1521.
Many people in the 1400s worshipped the god Tezcatlipoca – the divinity of smoke, darkness, hurricanes and destruction.

The Aztecs and Tezcatlipoca

During the great period of the Aztec Empire in the 1400s, a daily preoccupation for a great many people was worshipping and placating the god Tezcatlipoca, the one-legged divinity of smoke, darkness, hurricanes and destruction. A great many darkly beautiful representations of Tezcatlipoca were made by affixing precious stones to the skulls of people who had been sacrificed in his honour.

It was believed that when an earlier version of humanity had failed to worship him appropriately, the god had flown into a rage and unleashed a titanic storm that had annihilated everyone on Earth. To avoid such a catastrophe ever recurring, every year a young man – selected for his supposed likeness to Tezcatlipoca – would be sacrificed to the god and his remains eaten by priests and royalty. The testy deity would then be induced to send benign rains to end the dry season and implored to resist his more apocalyptic instincts.

These were deeply and sincerely held beliefs, propounded by the most learned people of the day. To doubt or disregard them would have been reckless. Of course, dangerous questions must, in secret, sometimes have crossed people's minds: how do we know Tezcatlipoca really exists? How do we know that he wants us to do these things? Nevertheless, to utter such heresies aloud would have been to invite imprisonment and death.

Today, Tezcatlipoca has no power to frighten anyone: he's a carefully labelled exhibit in a museum and a point of reference in obscure academic treatises on the history of weather deities. Our own attempts to predict rainfall involve sober investigations of surface ocean temperatures and the intensity of the currents of El Niño.

The beliefs about Tezcatlipoca have no possible basis in reality, but the Aztecs were not unusually credulous in holding them. On the contrary, measured against the broad span of history, they were entirely normal for doing so. All societies have collectively clung to peculiar ideas that were later revealed to be deeply mistaken and often close to insane. It would be impossible if the same were not true of our own times. The focus of mass delusion may change, but the phenomenon of delusion never abates. Central elements of beliefs that are now popularly taken to be the truth are almost certain to be mistaken because crowds are not interested in discovering the precise dimensions of reality. The hordes are not agitated by subtle lapses in reasoning; they don't urgently demand higher standards of evidence or march through the streets insisting on more thorough research. They merely want to find a sense of reassuring togetherness while demonising and shaming those who disagree with them.

Far from clearing the air, modern democracy plays straight into this tendency in our nature, equating the majority view with justice and righteousness. Markets, too, emphasise the primacy of popular sentiment by rewarding companies that have no inclination to disabuse their customers of their errors of taste. It's our strange fate to be born into an age of crowds in which the best, most precise thoughts are unlikely ever to meet with popular recognition.

Such an aristocratic attitude can sound absurdly outdated, but it offers us a vital idea – one which has nothing to do with genealogy or connections to the landed gentry. It's the idea of being convinced from the outset that popular opinion will frequently be riddled with errors and at odds with the beliefs of a thoughtful few, and that sanity must involve a willingness not to be ashamed, embarrassed or even much saddened at being repeatedly out of synch with the dominant culture.

By understanding without rancour why most people subscribe to the myths of any age, we are released from waging a hopeless and dispiriting struggle against public opinion. We don't expect our reasoned mentality to spread or to be easily absorbed; we know that most people will worship whatever version of Tezcatlipoca happens to be in vogue. Neither do we have to blame them. We can simply keep quietly to ourselves and hope never to end up on the wrong side of a sacrificial frenzy.

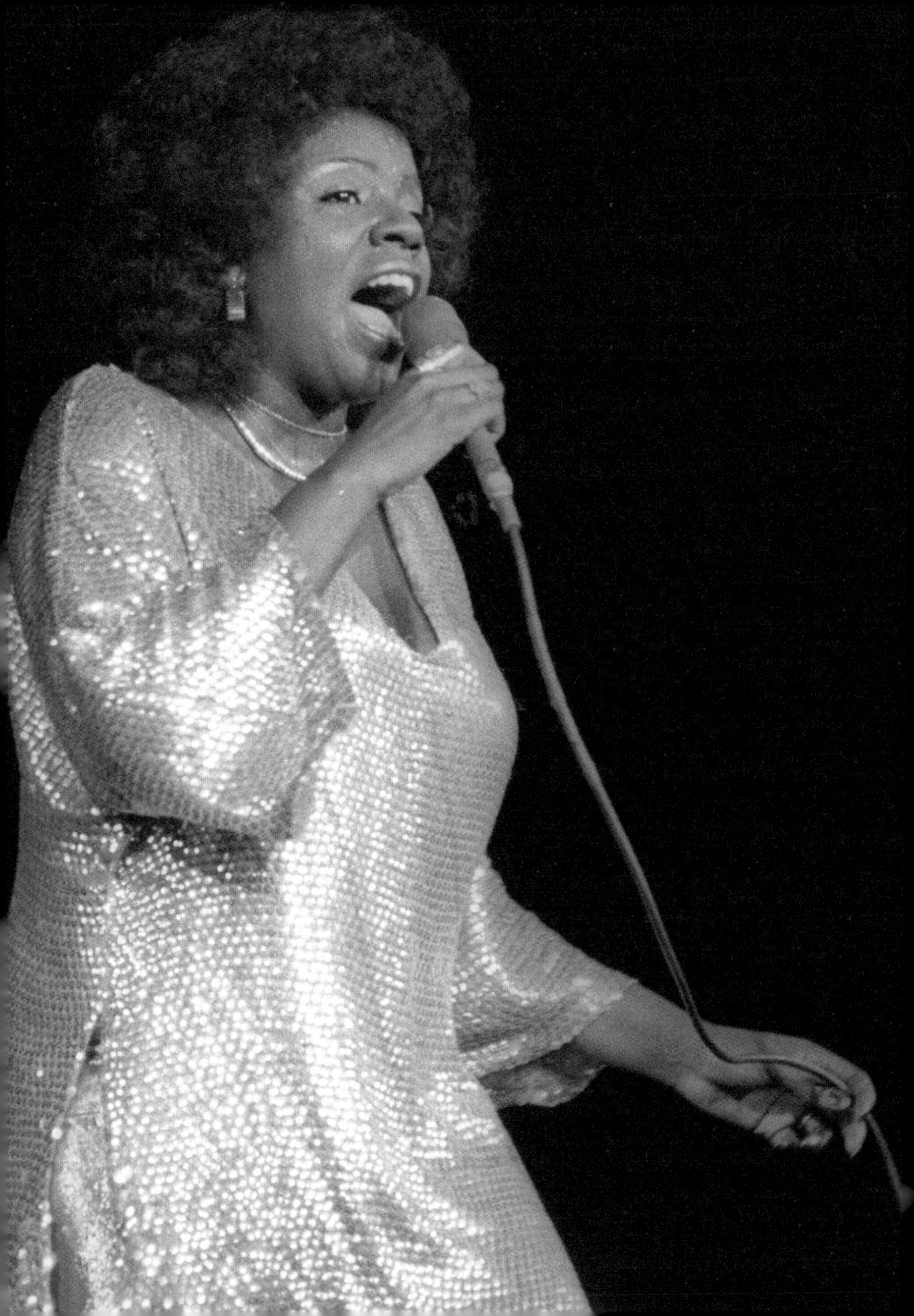

VIII.

Defiance

Gloria Gaynor singing 'I Will Survive', 1979, the lyrics of which instil the state of mind in which we can bear to take on those who have injured us.

'I Will Survive'

In October 1976, one of the greatest pop songs of the 20th century was heard for the first time: Gloria Gaynor's eternal assertion of defiance, 'I Will Survive'. It was initially released as a B-side, but it quickly became one of the bestselling singles of all time thanks to its power to touch something universal in the human soul.

Gloria Gaynor hadn't written the song herself. The words had, in fact, been penned by Dino Fekaris, a rather successful but temporarily disgruntled professional songwriter who'd just been sacked by Motown Records. The song is in part a recollection of being trampled upon and taken for granted, but it's not really about the wrong others have done to us; it's an honest appraisal of the way we have let them do these things to us, because we have been insufficiently on our own side:

> At first I was afraid, I was petrified
> Kept thinking I could never live
>   without you by my side

Others have undoubtedly harmed us, but the deeper problem is that we have not known how to esteem ourselves highly enough to stop them doing so. They thought that we would crumble and lay down and die, and they did so for good reason: because this is what we did so many times before. The beauty of the song is that it doesn't deny that we have been accomplices to our own bad treatment. We identify with its heroine because she is frank enough to admit that she has been the architect of her own humiliation.

We identify in Gloria the overcompliant, fearful part of ourselves. And it's because she understands our submissive tendencies so well that her deep encouragement to say a resolute 'fuck off' to the world is so rousing. This is not the voice of someone who has never been put upon; it is that of a weak and timid being who is no longer going to let her fears rule her life.

Defiance doesn't mean asserting that we *know* we will survive. At that moment when we belt out the song on the dance floor or (more likely) in the kitchen, we don't truly know what will happen to us and our fears are still raw. We may have been bullied throughout our relationships or our childhoods; we may only recently have instructed a lawyer to initiate divorce proceedings or written an email to a colleague. But when we join in joyfully with the chorus, we're making a great and precious leap of faith. We're finally insisting that our ability to cope is greater than our past has led us to imagine.

Gloria is backing us up to attain what we might term 'emotional escape velocity'. She's instilling in us, with the encouragement of deceptively simple yet mesmerising chords, the state of mind in which we can bear to take on those who have injured us.

An attitude of defiance is never the whole of what we need. For things to go well, we must also call on reserves of conciliation, compromise, acceptance and tolerance – the mature virtues by which genuinely good things are kept afloat in an imperfect world. But that's not where we are right now; at this point, we still need to gird ourselves for a fight. And this is when the voice of Gloria Gaynor is not just a magnificent instance in the grand history of pop; it is, for us (in a way it might feel embarrassing to admit to anyone else), the voice our soul needs to hear to save us from the weak but agonisingly familiar side of our nature that has so often given up too soon on our hopes of freedom.

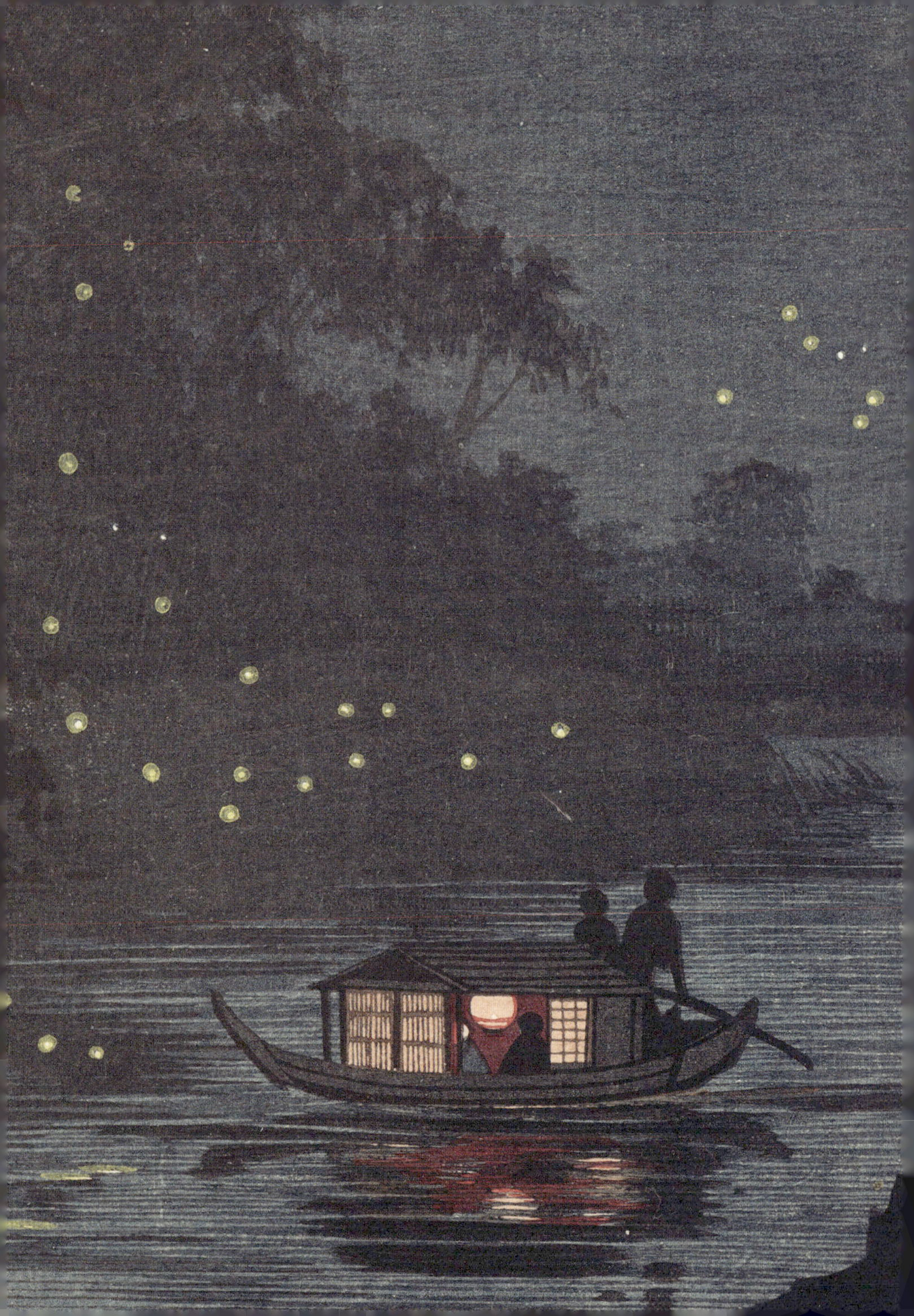

IX.

This too shall pass

Kobayashi Kiyochika, *Fireflies at Ochanomizu*, c. 1880 (detail).
We, too, are brief flickers of light in the darkness of the universe.

The *hotaru*

One of nature's odder creatures is the firefly: a soft-bodied beetle that emits a warm yellow glow from its lower abdomen, typically at twilight, in order to attract mates or prey. The firefly is a common sight in Japan, where it is known as the *hotaru*. Hotarus are at their most plentiful in June and July and can be seen buzzing in large groups around rivers and lakes. The glittering light is so enchanting that the Japanese have traditionally held firefly festivals – or *hotaru matsuri* – to watch the creatures caper and to recite poetry in their honour.

Something else has happened to the firefly in Japanese culture: it has become philosophical. Zen Buddhist poets and philosophers (the two terms here are largely interchangeable) have urged us to look at fireflies as sources of a distinctive wisdom and serenity. What we are being invited to see in the firefly is not an insect, but a version of ourselves. We too are tiny against the darkness, we too have no option but to put on a desperate light show in the hope of enticing possible partners and we too won't last very long (fireflies die within three weeks).

Importantly, the metaphor is a generous one. We're not being likened to rats or flies, with whom we share a few less flattering similarities as well. Fireflies are graceful and mesmerising. They appear bold and touching, protesting bravely against the blackness in the limited hours accorded to them.

Many of our bad moods and troubles spring from an overambitious sense of who we are. We ascribe to ourselves an importance that the natural world and our fellow humans turn out not to recognise. We protest in a bad temper at our perceived puniness and lack of agency.

The metaphor of the firefly bids us to loosen our hold on arrogance and irritation. We should not complain at our slightness; we should submit to it with wonder and poise. It isn't a personal curse that we won't live very long and that our actions are but a short, merry dance. We should know and accept our nature; a firefly should not mistake itself for a lion or a tortoise. It's possible to imagine our cities from outer space looking much like the frantic swirls of fireflies across a lake: touching, absurd, beautiful ... and miniscule within the order of the cosmos.

The Zen school of Buddhism repeatedly locates important philosophical themes in the natural world – for example, in relation to bamboo (evocative of resilience), water (a symbol of patient strength, capable of wearing down stone) and cherry blossoms (an emblem of the brevity of happiness). Zen seeks to hang its ideology on everyday things because it wants to make use of what is most ordinarily in our sight to keep us tethered to nourishing truths.

It also surrounds its lessons with poetry. In his legendary haiku, the great 17th-century poet Matsuo Basho attempts to quieten our egoistic ambition by focusing us on a firefly, through which we may grow more attentive to our own finitude:

> Falling from
> A blade of grass,
> to fly off –
> A firefly.

The firefly, on its slender wings, is the ideal reminder of a Zen belief in dignified resignation in the face of the mightiness and destructiveness of the natural order. Kobayashi Issa, an 18th-century Buddhist priest and haiku master, wrote 230 poems on fireflies. In one of the most celebrated, he captures a moment in high summer when time is momentarily stilled as the insects put on their show:

> The fireflies are sparkling
> And even the mouth of a frog
> Hangs wide open

It is a tiny moment of *satori*, or 'enlightenment'. The frog is as wonderstruck as the poet at the movements of the brave, doomed fireflies – much as we should be amazed, grateful and ultimately joyous to have been allocated a few brief moments in which to dance and flicker against the darkness of an impenetrable, 13.8-billion-year-old universe.

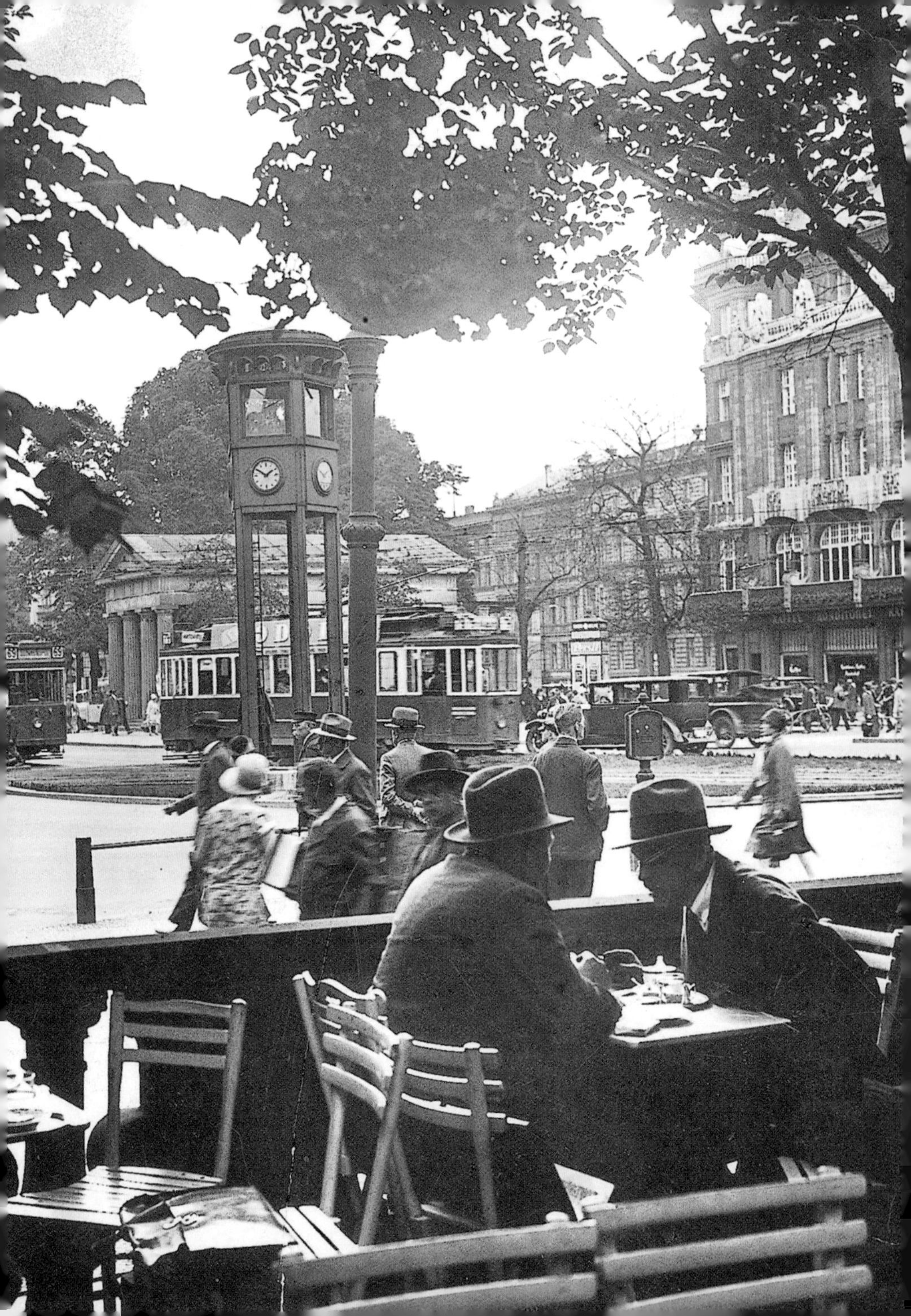

X.

Dust to dust

Berlin's Potsdamer Platz, as seen from Café Josty in 1930.

A single moment in time, now lost to history.

Berlin, spring 1930

In the spring of 1930, you could have visited the Café Josty and ordered a hot chocolate and a slice of sachertorte or a pear tart and a glass of Apollinaris sparkling water; a waiter in a black suit and bow tie might have tried to tempt you with an offer of an orange cake with poppy seeds. You would have had a good view onto the lively scene of Potsdamer Platz: plane trees, trams heading down Bellevuestrasse, students from the nearby Lycée Français walking purposefully to class, and at one corner, dominating Leipziger Strasse, Europe's largest department store, Wertheim – described by architectural critics as more ecclesiastical and awe-inspiring than Berlin Cathedral, both of which had been completed in 1897.

Then, in just a few years, everything in your immediate visual field would be gone: the newspaper stand, the trams, the trees. The waiter would have become a guard in an SS unit in Ukraine, one of the students would have been taken to Auschwitz-Birkenau, the Wertheim family would have been driven into exile and the trees chopped down for firewood. Waiting in the future was the Reichstag fire, Kristallnacht, the Sudetenland, Czechoslovakia, the end of Poland, Year Zero and the Wall, which would run through what had been the café and its legendary glass displays filled with chocolate and walnut cakes. History renders us ridiculous. We make plans, we opine on the future, we dare to imagine ourselves in control, we look at our diaries, we dutifully rise every day to work on our projects – and somewhere in the heavens, a malevolent angel looks on at the comedy and tries to stifle their guffaws. How little we have learnt from all that has collapsed before us – from the eradication of everything that stood where we do at the end of the Devonian period, the disappearance of all those tetrapods and stromatoporoids, trilobites and ammonites. We sip our coffees and eat our cakes and have the impudence to believe that the day ahead makes sense.

We can't know exactly what the disaster will be, whether it will strike only us or take down our whole society at the same time, but it is supercharging its energies even now. The only certainty is that nothing will endure. We are erecting matchstick houses on the sides of a roaring ocean.

Yet there is a degree of relief in the heartbreak. There is always so much pride and cruelty within the human edifice; the grand guest in the café cuts us dead, we are left off the invitation list, no one remembers us, our ambitions are frustrated. But we can be assured that these minor reversals will eventually be subsumed by the entropic forces that will sweep the whole comedy aside.

We have little option but to take every day seriously. We will get cross that we are delayed in traffic, that someone hasn't replied to our call and that a colleague is gossiping about us. Yet amidst our aggravations and humiliations, we can draw comfort from the sure knowledge of eventual darkness. Our enemies will be forgotten, the winners will be buried and the gossip will grow incomprehensible. The temples of the proud will be brought low and we will be at rest, the waters above us quieted. As it turns out, there is a sweet upside to the quiet contemplation – perhaps at a corner seat of a comfortable café – of our wholesale nullity in time and space and the absolute insignificance of every one of our self-important activities.

3.

Reasons of Light

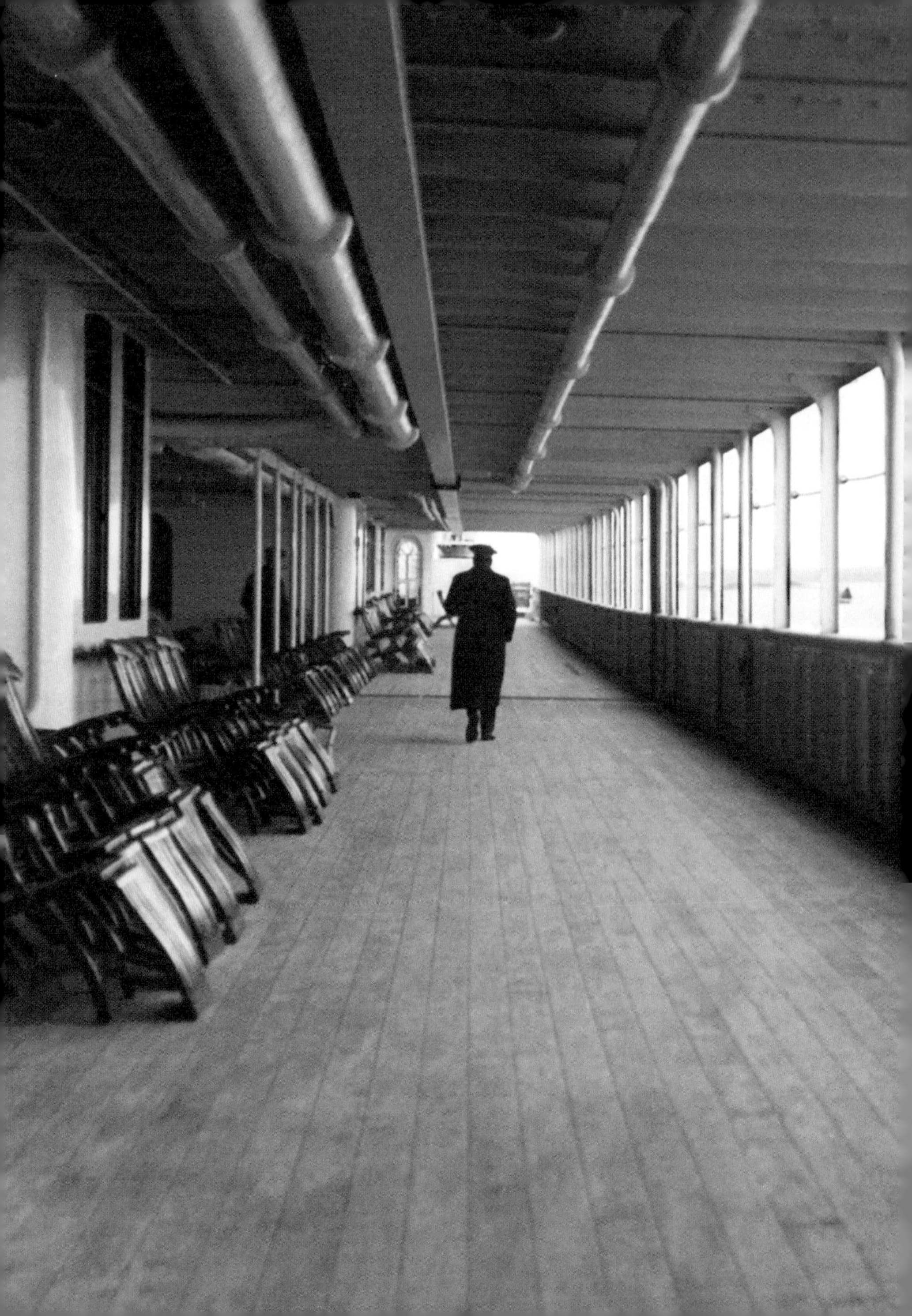

I.

There's still time to find joy

Titanic's port-side A-Deck promenade and its deckchairs. When our greater hopes for ourselves become impossible, we must grow inventive about the lesser options that remain.

The deckchairs on the *Titanic*

There remain few expressions better able to capture the futility of a task than to describe it as comparable to 'rearranging the deckchairs on the *Titanic*'. When the hull has been breached and the ship is sinking, to concern ourselves with the position of the loungers would be the ultimate folly, the deepest possible failure to recognise the true hopelessness of a situation.

The phrase seems grimly apt because we are a little like passengers on a stricken liner. Our greater hopes in life have been fatally ruptured: we see now that our career won't ever particularly flourish; our relationships will always be compromised; we've passed our peak in terms of looks; our bodies are going to fall prey to ever more humiliating illnesses; society isn't going to cure itself; significant political progress looks deeply improbable. Our ship is going down. It can feel as if trying to improve our condition, let alone find pleasure and distraction, would be an insult to the facts. Our instinct is to be as funereal and gloomy as our ultimate end.

But there's one crucial element that differentiates our predicament from that of the passengers who lost their lives on the RMS *Titanic* in the early hours of 15th April

1912: *time*. They had little more than two hours between the moment they felt the ominous shudder of impact and the moment when the once-majestic vessel broke apart and sank into the North Atlantic. We're going down, too – but far, far more slowly. It's as if the captain has let it be known that the hull has been breached, there are no lifeboats and there is zero chance of ever reaching port – but has added that it will probably be many decades before we actually slip beneath the waves.

So, though we can't be saved, and though the end will be grim, we still have options as to how to use our remaining time. We might be involved in a catastrophe, but there are better and worse ways to fill the days. In the circumstances, expending thought and effort on 'rearranging the deckchairs' is no longer ridiculous at all; it's an eminently logical step.

When our greater hopes for ourselves become impossible, we must grow inventive in the lesser options that remain. Keeping cheerful and engaged, in spite of everything, becomes a major task. If we were on a very gradually sinking luxury liner in the early 20th century, we might strive to put on a dinner jacket every evening and go and dance the foxtrot to the music of the string quintet, sing a cheerful song or settle into the second-class library on

C Deck – as, all the while, bits of seaweed and debris lapped at our ankles. Or we might look out for the best spot for our collapsible recliner so that we could watch the seabirds wheeling in the sky, or gain some privacy for a long, soul-exploring conversation with a new friend – to the sound of crockery smashing somewhere in a galley down below. We might alternatively try our first game of quoits on the slightly tilting deck or drop in – contrary to our habits up to this time – on a wild party in steerage. Of course, our lives would – from a wider perspective – remain a thorough disaster, but we might find we were starting to enjoy ourselves.

Such inventiveness is precisely what we must learn to develop to cope with our state. How can we invest the coming period with meaning even though everything is, overall, entirely dark? It's a question our culture hasn't prepared us for. We've been taught to focus on our big hopes, on how we can aim for everything going right. We crave a loving marriage, deeply satisfying and richly rewarding work, a stellar reputation, an ideally fit body and positive social change. We've not yet been prepared to ask ourselves what remains when many of these are no longer available; when love will always be tricky, politics compromised or the crowd hostile. What are our viable versions of the best spot for a deckchair on a listing liner?

If marriage is far less blissful than we'd imagined, perhaps we can turn to friendship; if society won't accord us the dignity we deserve, perhaps we can find a group of fellow outcasts; if our careers have irretrievably faltered, perhaps we can turn to new interests; if political progress turns out to be perennially blocked and the news is always sour, we might absorb ourselves in nature or history.

In this approach, we turn to what our society might dismiss as 'plan Bs' – what you do when you can't do the things you really want to do. But here's the thing: it may turn out that the secondary, lesser, lighter reasons for living are, in fact, more substantial than we'd imagined. And once we get to know them, we might come to think that they are what we should have been focused on all along – only it has taken a seeming disaster for us to realise how central they should always have been.

1493

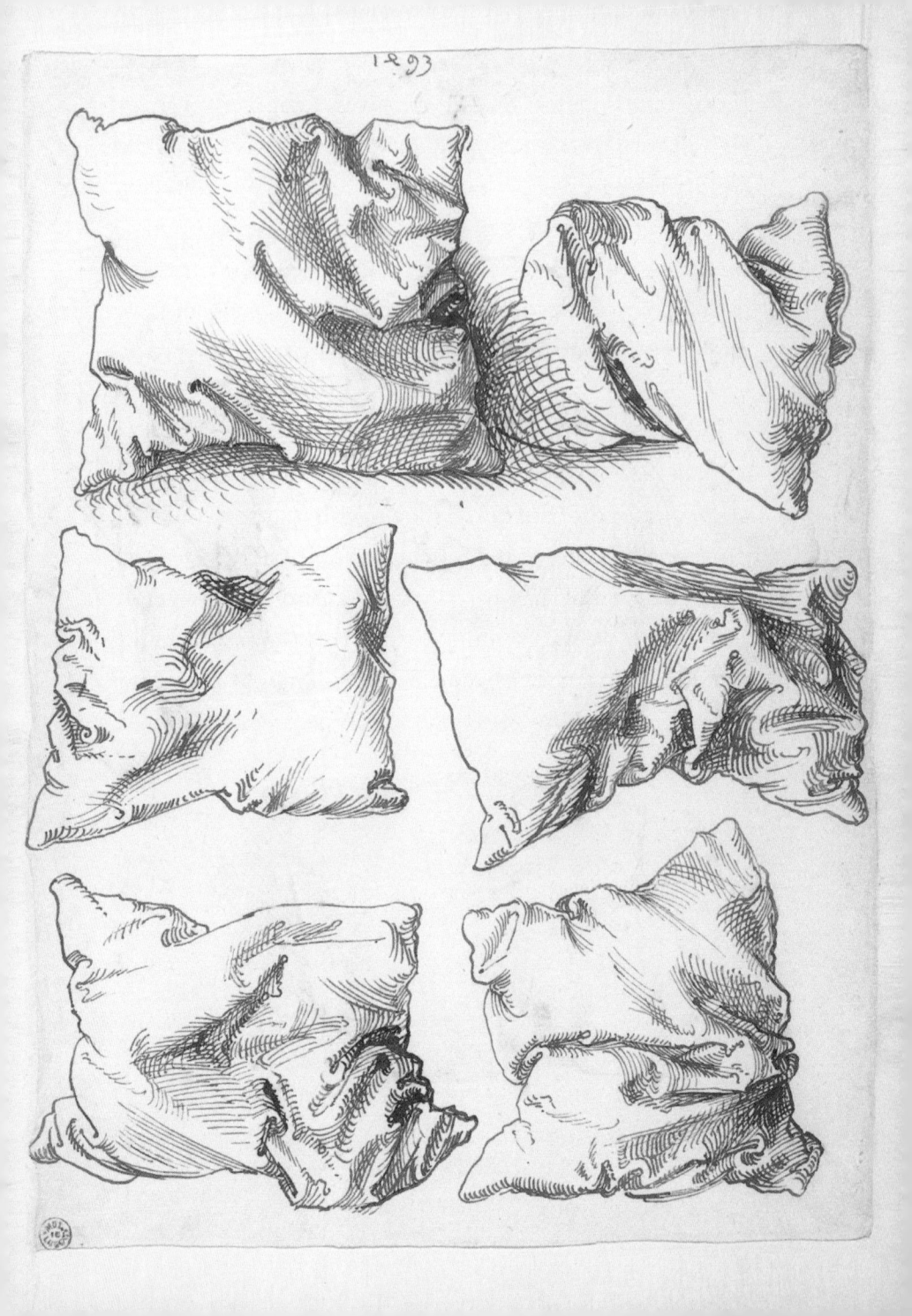

II.

Small pleasures

Albrecht Dürer, *Six Studies of Pillows*, 1493. Pillows so often and so generously receive our tears in the wake of our disappointments.

Albrecht Dürer and his pillows

One of the most beautiful and unexpectedly moving sketches in the world was completed by the German artist Albrecht Dürer in 1493, when he was 22 years old and apprenticed in his native Nuremberg. It shows six pillows, probably his own, in a variety of shapes and positions.

On the other side of the paper, Dürer drew himself, looking at us with penetration and inquisitiveness, alongside a version of his hand, and at the bottom, for good measure, another (seventh) pillow.

A pillow has no distinguished place in the order of the universe. We are unlikely ever to have paid much attention to this modest household object. We take its existence for granted, owing it no special gratitude and unlikely to have ever been detained by its qualities. Like so much else that we are surrounded by, we see it without noticing it; it belongs to a vast category of things that we rely on without for an instant stopping to wonder at, or derive any satisfaction from. We are, for the most part, wholly blind.

In the face of our customary inattention, it helps us greatly that a long time ago a genius arrested his gaze in order to tell us that, among the neglected detritus of a household,

Albrecht Dürer, *Self-portrait, Study of a Hand and a Pillow*, 1493

there might be something worth bothering with – that a pillow properly considered might be as interesting as a castle or as nuanced as a poem; that we have all along been putting our heads down on a treasury.

It matters, too – though ideally it shouldn't – that Dürer's work is highly acclaimed. The pillow image is stored in a special temperature-controlled room in New York's Metropolitan Museum of Art, it has been the subject of extensive study by elaborately trained art historians and it would cost more than a sports car were it ever to be put on sale. We are by nature immoderately snobbish creatures; we appreciate principally those few things that the most prestigious voices in society have excited us to be curious about – which means we spend a lot of time thinking about fame and glory, and no time at all attending to most of what lies closest to us, which includes not just our pillows, but also the lemon on the sideboard, the light at dusk, an afternoon free of commitments, the flowers in the garden, the laughter of a child, the kindness of a friend, a history book on the shelf and the many small moments of harmony and satisfaction that, despite our many difficulties, we have already witnessed.

Dürer was one of the most acclaimed artists of the European Renaissance and lends us his immense prestige in order that we might in turn learn to draw pleasure from thoroughly unprestigious things. We may declare our lives to be worthless and cast envious glances at the achievements of our rivals, but all along we trample on what keener, more alert eyes would know how to feast on.

Throughout his career, Dürer looked at ordinary life and saw it for the improbably ecstatic, jewel-filled pantheon it is. A few years after the pillows, he completed a study of a range of ordinary plants and grasses, wondering at the capacity of the smallest clod of earth to give life to so much beauty and interest.

Nothing could be further from the realm of worldly ambition than a bunch of columbines; such flowers grow freely in any stony, seemingly unpromising soil. There's no market in them, no one has ever boasted of owning what is more or less a weed. But for Dürer, such spectacles of nature were among the most serious sources of pleasure that exist, worth as much as a coat of arms and more likely to satisfy us than a love affair. He relished the delicacy of shoots; he admired the individuality of petals and the subtle colours of new leaves. Fulfilment – which we are taught exists only in a good reputation, financial achievement and costly decorative objects – may be already here, waiting for us in a crack in the pavement or a window box.

Albrecht Dürer, *Columbine*, 1495–1500

We may not have Dürer's talent, but in this instance we don't need it. We're not trying to become artists; we're trying to become people who have reasons to be hopeful. And in this regard, Dürer is generous. He reminds us that there are reasons everywhere – in the way the light falls on a cup, in a few words with someone who still cares about us, in a banana cake we might make tomorrow. The lesson is not to focus on exactly the same things that Dürer studied (though we might do this, too); it's to take his attitude of generosity, openness and modesty and apply it to our own circumstances. We might find our version of his satisfaction in a pattern of lichen on an old stone wall or in the refined elegance of a boiled egg.

So compelling was Dürer's skill as an artist that he came to the notice of the rich and powerful, including the Holy Roman Emperor Maximilian I. Maximilian loved horses, wars, armour and pageantry. Most of all, he loved himself, for all the important things he had done (expanding the Habsburg dynasty to Spain, recapturing Austria, checking the power of the French). He asked Dürer if he might make a work of art that would celebrate his achievements, his character and his place in history, and urged him to make it as big as possible. Money was no object. The result was one of the largest prints ever made: 3 metres high, on thirty-six sheets of paper, from 195 woodblocks.

Albrecht Dürer, *Triumphal Arch*, c. 1515

The central arch was called 'Honour', the right arch 'Nobility' and the left arch 'Praise'. Each one was densely packed with illustrations highlighting Maximilian's wisdom, courage, strength, popularity and good nature. In one area, there was a complicated family tree that traced his lineage back to Clovis I, the first king of the Franks, and in another, a table that equated his achievements with Julius Caesar and Alexander the Great.

Maximilian was delighted. He praised Dürer to all the aristocracy and had copies of the work delivered to every corner of his lands. But the artist was less content; he had done it for the money and his heart wasn't remotely in such bombast. Too much in his character went in other directions: towards the everyday, towards humility and towards an awareness of how disaster might strike each one of us, even or especially the mighty ones, at any moment.

Dürer's mind was dominated by terrifying visions of what fate might have in store: disease, famine, injustice and war laying waste to dreams and ambitions. In his self-portraits, he never disguised his anxiety. In a second early work, he shows himself holding a shrivelled thistle, a symbol of pain, decay and defeat. His look of suspicion and wariness is directed not at us, but at himself. He knew how quickly, and with how few wrong moves, we can all be undone.

Albrecht Dürer, *The Four Horsemen*, from the *Apocalypse*, 1498

Albrecht Dürer, *Portrait of the Artist Holding a Thistle*, 1493

Ruin or disgrace may well catch up with us. Things collapse and plans turn sour (shortly after the arch was completed, Maximilian fell into a depression and, inconsolable, insisted on sleeping in and being carried around all day in a coffin; he died four years later). But we don't need everything to succeed for existence to be bearable; we can survive and thrive through a disciplined focus on those smaller elements around us that lie more reliably within our command and which offer us pleasure without exacting envy or punishing effort. We can nourish ourselves on the sight of flowers, on the smell of freshly baked bread, on an evening writing our diary or on a walk around the park. We can take pleasure in an apricot, in a hot bath, in some flowering weeds – and, not least, in our own set of pillows that have so often and so generously received our tears in the wake of our disappointments.

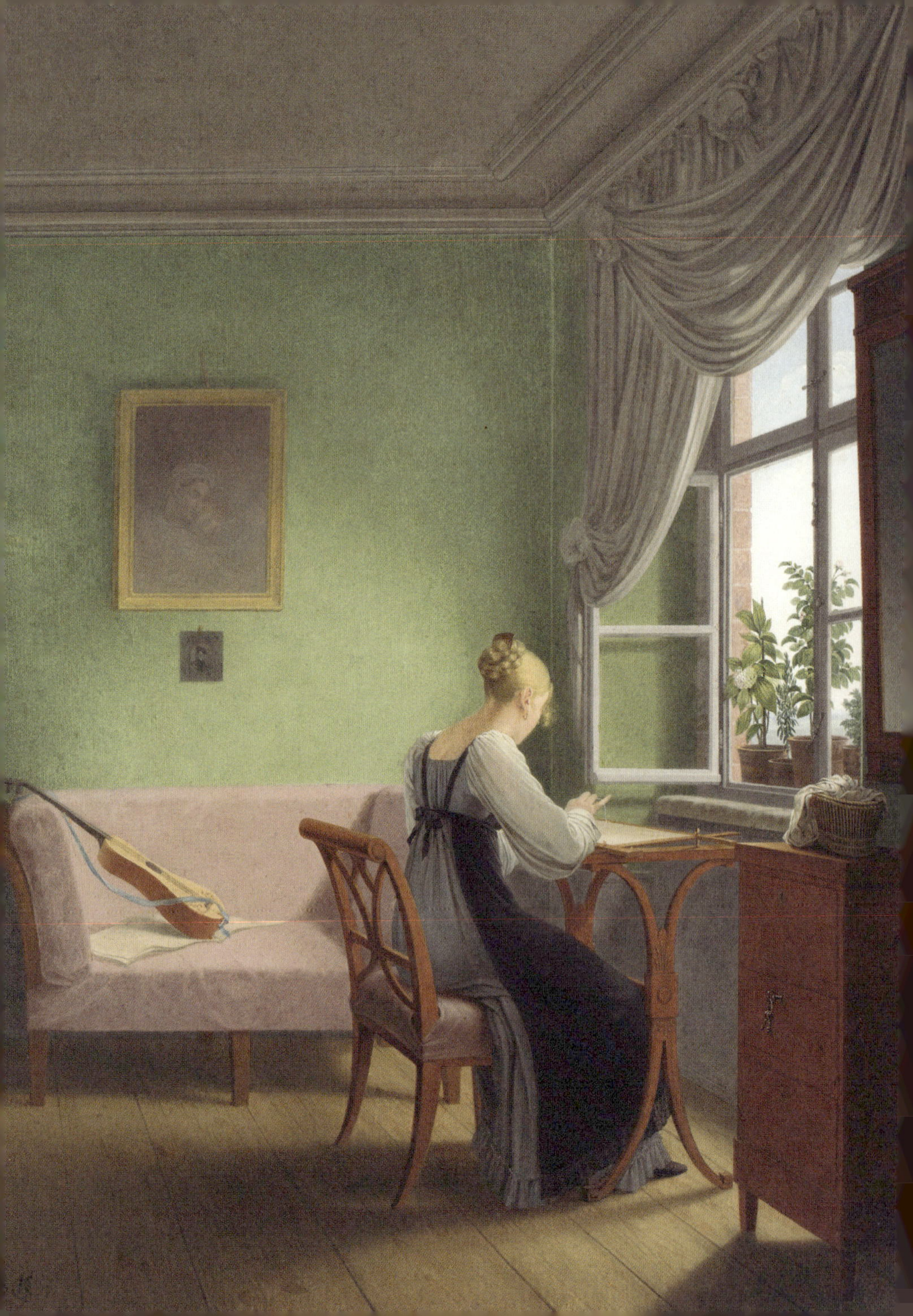

III.

The consolations of home

Georg Friedrich Kersting, *The Embroiderer*, 1817. We should gain security from understanding how much our home can shore up our moods.

Kersting and lamplight

We might be tempted to feel rather sorry for someone who confesses that their greatest pleasure in life is staying at home – or, worse still, that their deepest satisfactions spring from interior design. What would need to have gone wrong for someone to prefer their own bedroom or kitchen to the theatres and clubs, parties and conference venues of the world? How narrow would someone's horizons need to have grown for them to devote hours to choosing a flower-ringed vase for the sideboard or a brass lamp for the study? Our era has a hard time maintaining sympathy for domesticity. Reality lies outside our doors. There are really only two categories of people who can be forgiven for being heavily invested in staying at home: small children and losers.

But after launching our ambitions on the high seas, trying for a few decades to make a mark on our times and exhausting ourselves by sucking up to those in power and coping with gossip, slander and scandal, we might start to think less harshly of those who prefer to remain proudly within their own walls, thinking about cushions and jugs, pencil pots and garlic crushers, laundry cupboards and cleaning products.

It might, of course, be preferable to bend the world to one's own will, to tidy up the minds of millions or to fashion a business in one's image, but after a little time on the planet, many of us may be ready to look with new understanding and admiration at those who can draw satisfaction from making blackberry jam, planting beds of lavender or waxing bedroom floors.

The painter Georg Friedrich Kersting was born in northern Germany in 1785, and as a young man he wanted to become a great military general and perform heroic deeds in battle. He dreamt of helping to expel the French armies, which under Napoleon occupied large areas of the German states. After briefly studying art in Copenhagen, Kersting joined the Lützowsche Freikorps, a Prussian volunteer force, and saw action at the Battle of the Göhrde, in which thousands lost their lives and for which he received the Iron Cross for bravery.

But after the defeat of Napoleon, during the political impasse that befell the German states, something changed in Kersting. He retired from the military, gave up on politics, moved to Dresden, got married, had some children – and became very interested in the idea of 'home'.

Kersting had had enough of the machinations of government and the schemes of generals, of German nationalism and wars of liberation. Such ventures and the ideals that supported them became bound up in his mind with hubris and overreach. He was haunted by the bloodletting that he had witnessed and the friends from the military he had lost. From now on, what would interest him was the challenge of leading a good enough ordinary life in domestic circumstances, and of remaining sane and serene when there was so much that might unbalance and perturb one. He closed the door on the world and became a prophet of the consolations and beauty of home.

In 1817, Kersting completed one of the most quietly remarkable and beguiling paintings of the 19th century. *The Embroiderer* shows a young woman in a dignified, modest dress absorbed in her work at an open window. We cannot see her face, but we can imagine her lips pursed in concentration, her little finger on her right hand extended and taut from the effort of threading her needle. The interior is peaceful and inviting, without being in any way showy or extravagant. Someone has thought hard about how the mauve sofa will create an intriguing contrast with the green wallpaper, and the chunky wooden floorboards have been matched up with an especially graceful chair and table, suggesting a reconciliation between practicality and elegance. A few years later, Kersting completed an equally iconic companion piece. This time it is night and a woman is again at work doing some darning. A lamp has been swung into place and the room is bathed in a soft light; soon it will be time to make some camomile tea, kiss somebody on the forehead and rearrange their blankets and then, gradually, go to bed. The task isn't distinguished or obviously memorable, there will be no government medals or honours handed out as thanks for it, but through Kersting's eyes, we're in no doubt that something very special is going on. The sitter has been cast as a secular saint of a new, home-focused creed, which rejects prevailing assumptions about where glory might lie and what must count as intelligent and purposeful. Perhaps those who focus on the home will not gain distinction or renown, and their graves will not commemorate any obviously glittering deed, but they will nevertheless have played a role in supporting civilisation. It is to misunderstand where satisfaction lies to insist that fulfilment can only exist in cabinet rooms and boardrooms, stock markets and opera houses; the more imaginative will know the distinctive pleasures of preparing a family meal or painting a room, hanging a new picture or filling a vase with hyacinths and lilies of the valley.

We might once have wanted to tame and educate the entire world, to have had millions of people agree with us and to

Georg Friedrich Kersting, *Young Woman Sewing by Lamplight*, 1823

gain the adulation of strangers. But such plans are inherently unstable and open to being destroyed by envy and vanity. We should instead gain security from understanding how much a devotion to home can shore up our moods if our wider surroundings grow hostile. When we have become a laughing stock or when no one wants to know us any more, we can reactivate our dormant appreciation of our surroundings and find meaning in nothing greater or smaller than sewing on a few buttons in the late evening or choosing a new fabric for a chair. Kersting was not naïve, he understood how war, politics and business worked, but it was precisely because he did so that he was keen to throw his spotlight elsewhere. His art was political in the deepest sense, in that it articulated a vision of how one could ideally live: it covertly criticised military generals and emperors, business leaders and actors. Kersting's art shows us that waving flags at rallies and sounding important at meetings is well and good, but that the true battles are really elsewhere, in the trials of ordinary existence; that what counts as a proper victory is an ability to remain calm in the face of provocation – not to despair and not to give way to bitterness, but to vanquish paranoia, to decode one's own mind and to pay due attention to passing moments of grace.

Georg Friedrich Kersting, *Man Reading by Lamplight*, 1814

Kersting spent much time in his own study, which he represented in a number of sketches and in one especially famous painting. He must sometimes have regretted his old ambitions. It must have hurt that he never made a fortune and that he remained, in his lifetime, relatively undiscovered. There might have been days when he felt that he had made all the wrong choices.

Nevertheless, his art continues to be a point of reference for those who have had enough of trying to bring order to the public square. It urges us to accept the consolation and peace available in ceasing to worry what others think and in learning to limit our ambitions to the boundaries of our own dwellings and laundry cupboards.

Tonight, we might choose to stay in, do some reading, finish patching a hole in a cardigan or try a new place for the armchair, and be intensely grateful that we have overcome the wish to live too much in the minds of strangers.

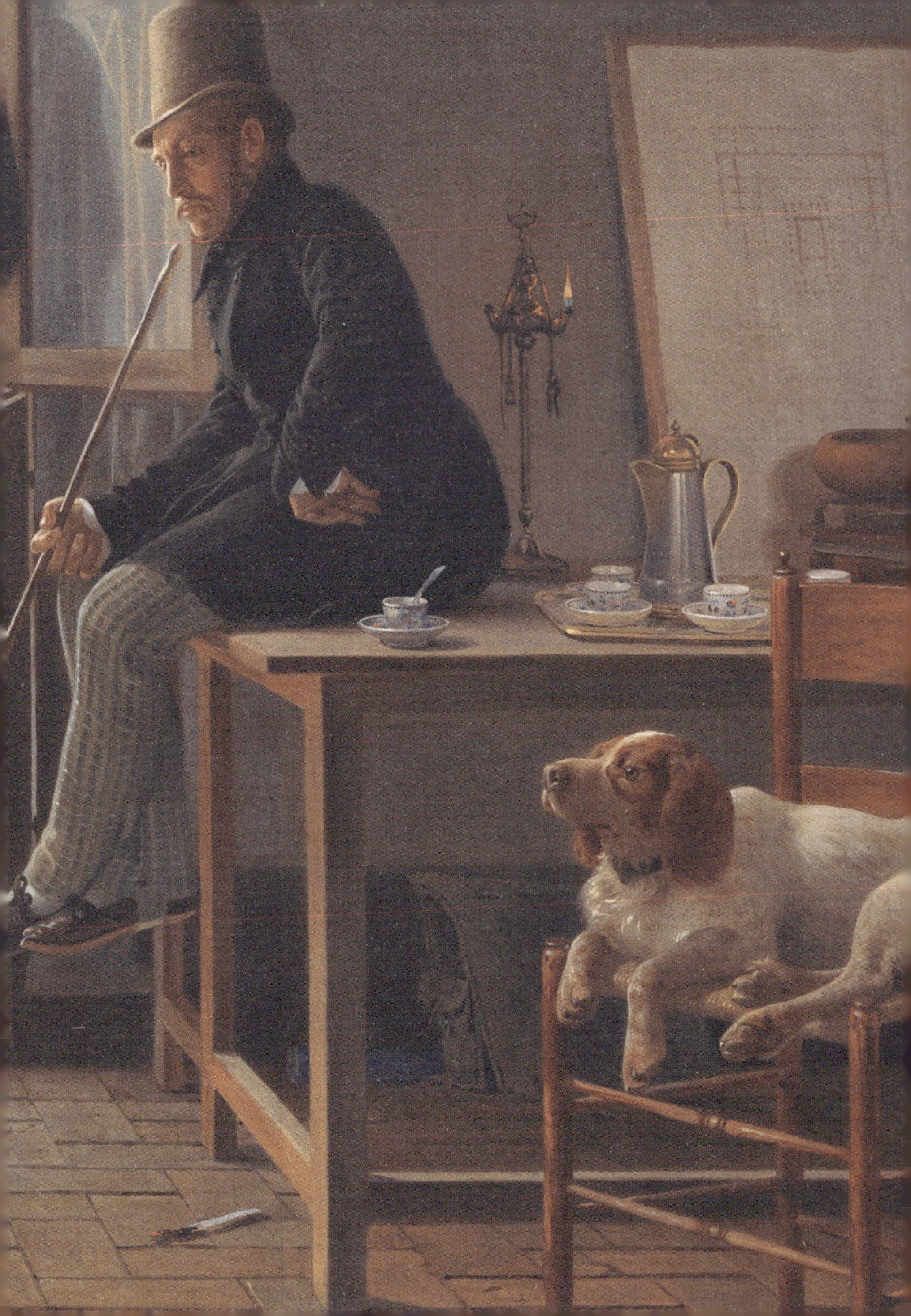

IV.

Friends

Constantin Hansen, *A Group of Danish Artists in Rome*, 1837 (detail).
We should all embrace the comfort offered by genuine friends.

Danish artists in Rome

In our lives, we start off by hoping that we will be liked by everyone. We aspire to broad popularity. It's hardly surprising: we evolved as group creatures, dependent for their survival on the approval of all the other members in their small roving band of hunter-gatherers. A single hostile acquaintance could have been the harbinger of physical attack. We can't help but instinctively worry ourselves sick about what others think of us.

Yet in the febrile conditions of modernity, it is close to impossible to get through life without attracting enemies. However polite and well-meaning we may be, however much we might incline to conciliation and gentleness, somewhere along the way we will slip up in a way that threatens to attract terrifying levels of hostility and mockery. Wholly unwittingly, we might upset someone who tried to get into a relationship with us; our success might elicit envy; our politeness might be mistaken for superciliousness; our kindness might be read as piety. A rumour that we are unprogressive in our opinions might spread in the workplace. Nothing needs to have gone especially wrong for us to find ourselves in social exile.

It's this instability that necessitates an appreciation for the value of that ultimate protection against groupthink and mob rule: the friend. We cannot rely upon the sanity of the crowd; instead we have to focus our efforts on the goodwill and sympathy of a few extremely carefully chosen souls.

In this regard, we might contemplate a picture of seven close friends (and a dog) painted in the 1830s by the Danish artist Constantin Hansen. At first glance, it looks like a pretty rendition of a contented circle relaxing at an open window in one of the most beautiful cities in Europe. But there is a darker aspect to Hansen's work. This wasn't just a portrait of friendship (though it was that, too); it was an evocation of the toll that can be imposed on free spirits by the narrow-mindedness and prejudice of society at large; its deeper message was intended for the judgemental bourgeoisie back in Denmark, for whom these people weren't lovable oddities but shocking outcasts. Carl Christian Constantin Hansen had gone to Rome to escape financial pressures after his parents' death. The painting shows him in his studio (sitting on the far left) chatting with Danish friends who were all, like him, misfits in one way or another. His friend Albert Küchler – standing in the middle of the balcony – was in the process of becoming a Catholic, an absurd step in the eyes of his family back home. Next to

Constantin Hansen, *A Group of Danish Artists in Rome*, 1837

him, in the white trousers, is Ditlev Blunck, who had to live in exile because his homosexuality was regarded as scandalous in Denmark. And sitting on the table is Jørgen Sonne, who had exited a respectable career in the military, in which his enthusiasm for Hindu spirituality wasn't viewed as an asset.

To a contemporary Danish audience, they would have been read as a weird, scandalous group with no care for earning money or leading regular, pious lives. The things they cared about sharply flouted the expectations of respectable minds. And yet, the way Hansen depicts them lets us feel, even in our own time, the comfort offered by kindly mutual regard. Whatever they were saying in the townhouses and Bible-reading classes of Copenhagen, in a studio in Rome, there was sympathy and communion. Friendship had defeated gossip.

We may not be talented artists in flight from our punishing provincial Protestant backgrounds, but we are liable in some ways to have upset, or to be in danger of upsetting, the judgements of our own era. We should not be too surprised if we have excited hatred; lunacy and delusion are the general rules. The only escape lies in identifying a number of people (we'd be extremely lucky if it was seven, but even one or two will do) who won't judge us by the standards of the day, who won't require us to have a certain kind of career, to obey particular principles in our personal lives or to espouse fashionable opinions about politics or class. We will have in them a bulwark against the pitiless massed guardians of truth and justice outside the door. We will be able to be ourselves and still be considered with love.

We have suffered long enough from hoping that sanity and kindness might be widespread. It should by now have grown evident that the mind of the average person is too hostile a place for us to flourish, and that we must sharply edit those whose judgement we will let ourselves be affected by. Once we have given up on the poisonous goal of respectability, we will at last be ready for friendship – and, if we are especially lucky, the companionship of a highly cordial-looking spaniel.

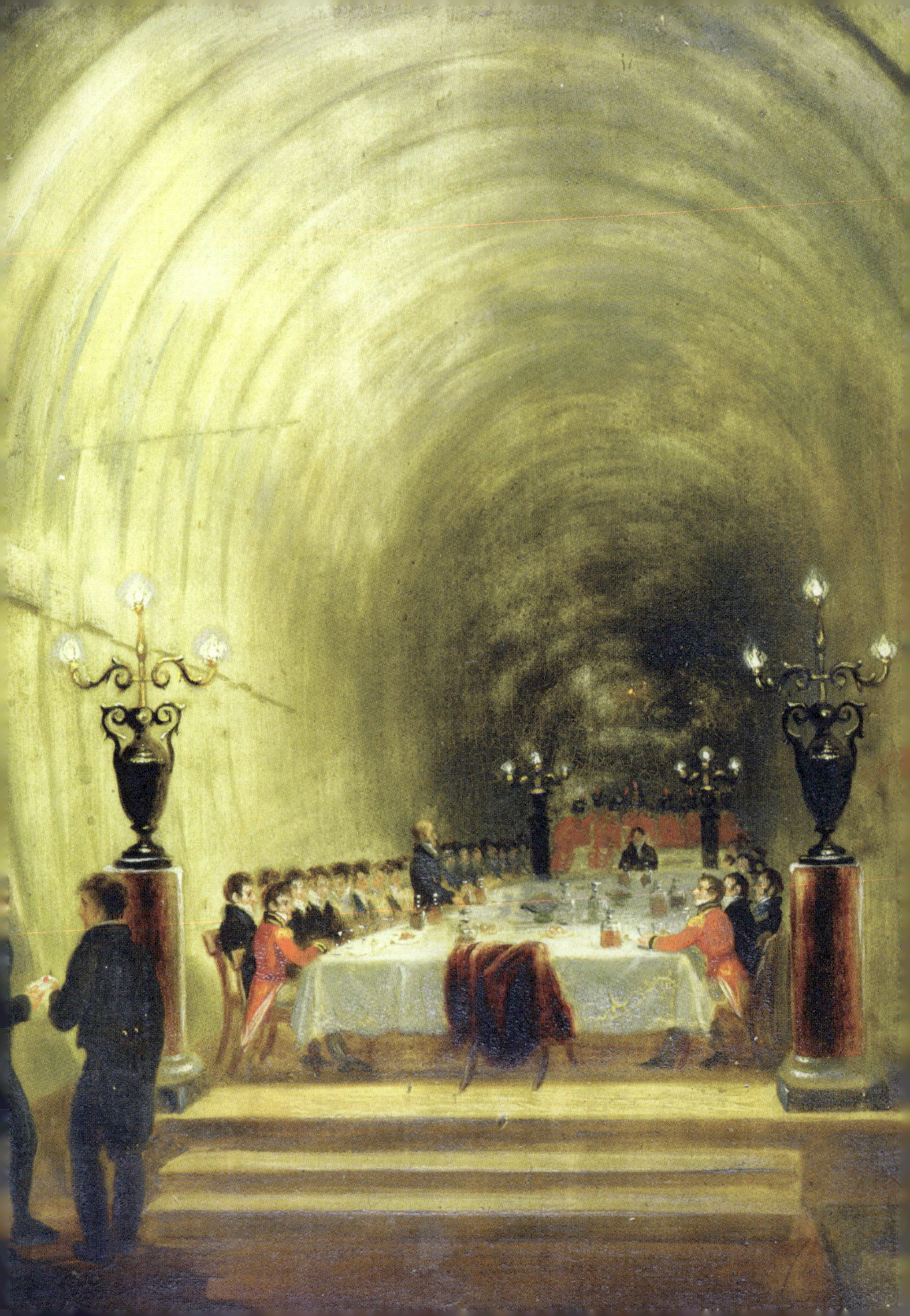

v.

The beauty of industry

George Jones (attr.), *Banquet in the Thames Tunnel*, c. 1827.
We should pause to admire everyday examples of engineering
and science we too often overlook.

A banquet under the Thames

On the evening of 10th November 1827, a much-publicised banquet was held in London. What set it apart from the many other festivities of the social season was the fact that it took place deep underground, in the first completed section of the first tunnel ever built under the River Thames.

It was a glamorous affair. Fifty guests sat down at a huge table illuminated by gas chandeliers; the place of honour was occupied by the greatest celebrity of the day, the victor at the Battle of Waterloo, the Duke of Wellington; patriotic songs were sung and at midnight a shovel and a pickaxe were brought in and a toast was drunk to the labourers involved in the construction of what was recognised as a marvel of art and science. The whole event was commemorated in a painting, commissioned from one of the most fashionable and popular artists of the era. Over the next few days, tens of thousands of people not fortunate enough to be on the invitation list had the chance, for a modest fee, to descend the shaft and admire the beautiful vaulting and elegant detailing of a new transport link.

Considering the event from our own vantage point, one might be struck by how little of this we do today. We, too, are surrounded by wonders of engineering and design, but we no longer give toasts in honour of bridges, pause to wonder at the alloy fan blades of our airplane engines, notice our transmission towers, pay homage to power stations or even register our door handles.

For most of history, it was very different. The Romans were profoundly impressed by their road systems and the mechanics of their water supply; their engineering projects were a logical focus of their cultural pride. In 18th-century Venice, the Arsenale di Venezia – for centuries the world's largest shipbuilding yard – was a major attraction; tourists came in large numbers to watch ships being assembled and repaired. An especially well-heeled visitor might even take home a memento in the form of a painting of the yard by the priciest of contemporary artists, Canaletto. Art was in the service of engineering, not the other way around.

In the 19th century, the admiring prophet of modernity, Walt Whitman, revealed his awe at the care that had gone into fashioning technological civilisation:

> Shapes of factories, arsenals, foundries, markets
> Shapes of the two-threaded tracks of railroads
> Shapes of the sleepers of bridges, vast frameworks,
>   girders, arches.

Canaletto, *View of the Entrance to the Arsenal, Venice,* 1732–1735

Our technology is yet more impressive, but our powers of appreciation have been reduced to nothing. It would be deeply unusual, even suspicious, to pause and admire the bold sweep of a concrete bridge over an alpine valley. Civilised people aspire to appreciate the great works of philosophy. Very few know or even care that a distinguished philosopher happened also to design an exemplary set of radiators and door handles, which he thought far surpassed the intelligence of his better-known work, *Tractatus Logico-Philosophicus*.

If this neglect matters, it is because it is perilously easy to give up on human beings when we consider ourselves only in terms of what we get up to in politics or our private lives, in warfare or ecology. The evidence from our news media is of insistent mania, querulousness, cruelty and self-absorption. We would have so many reasons to turn away from our species in lasting disgust.

If we want to keep a little faith in our own kind, however, it is possible to look elsewhere. In an average elevator, for example, lies a powerful covert argument against depression and misanthropy. This machine may never attract notice or praise, yet it is a summit of achievement in the quality, thoughtful dedication that went into making it. In the background of a plain ascending and descending

A door handle designed by Ludwig Wittgenstein, 1928

box is a grand history of science and mechanics and an astonishing system of regulation and care that ensures that we can be safely transported in seconds down to the vault-like concrete garage or up to the observation deck at the touch of a button.

Likewise, while a commercial port isn't currently on any of our lists of places to visit, it should be recognised as a sublime result of a vast creative and organisational collective effort. Similar wonder can be applied to the operating theatre of a hospital, a research laboratory, the loading bay of a supermarket, a sewage plant, an electricity substation, a motorway intersection, an airport control tower, a factory assembly line or an underground station.

There is every reason to be appalled by our race. But to retain a vestige of hope, we should look not at our books or our articles, our laws or our economic forecasts, our film award ceremonies and campaigns for justice, but at our docksides and warehouses, at our circuit boards and surgical instruments, at our flyovers and radar stations. Here, away from all grandstanding and sentimentality, viciousness and hard-heartedness, remain a host of convincing reasons to remain very proud of being human.

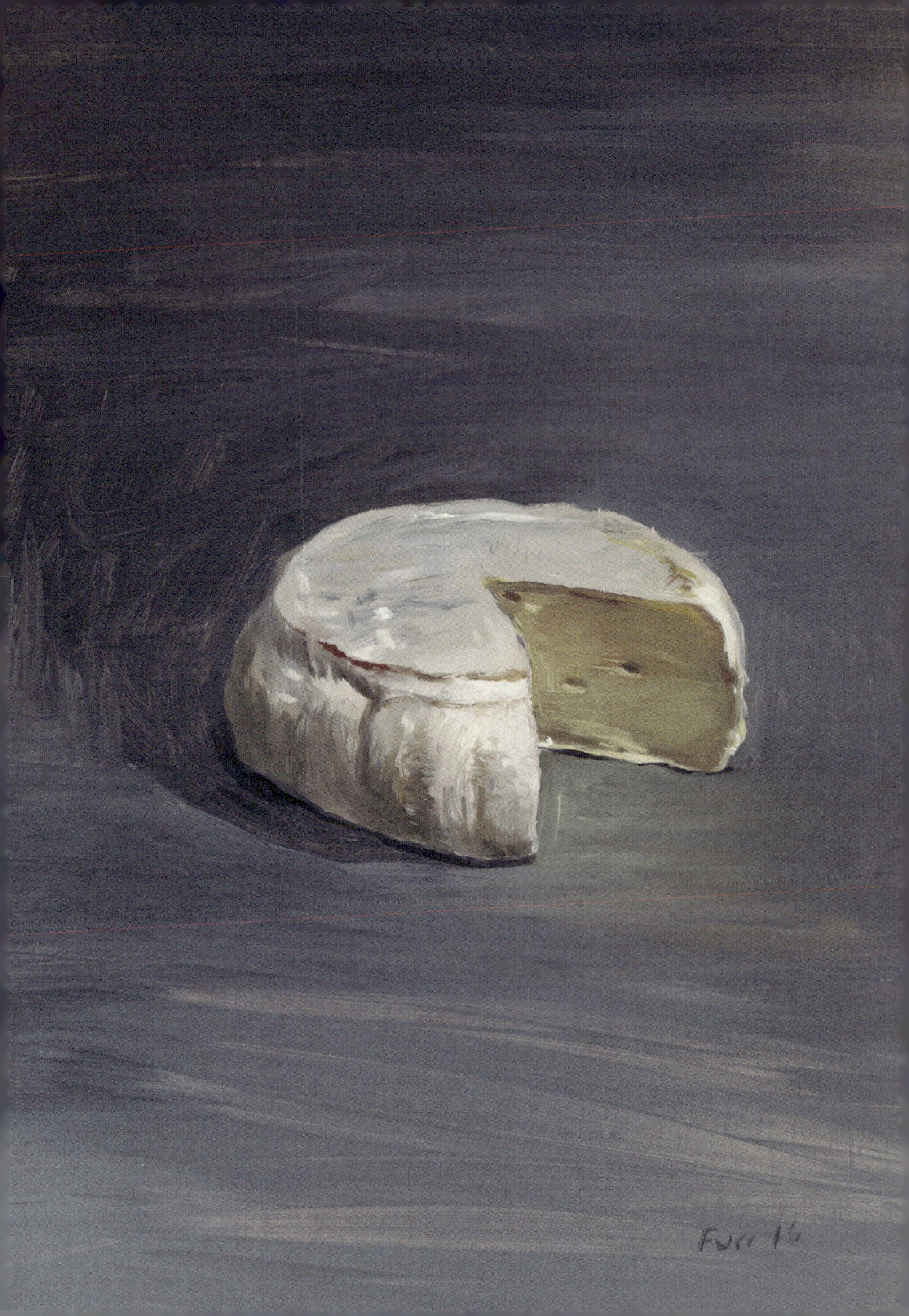
Furr 16

VI.

Reasons that bypass reason

Christian Furr, *Petit Reblochon on Midnight Blue*, 2016 (detail). A delicate and tantalising cheese can form a powerful reason to stay hopeful.

Reblochon cheese

When we think of reasons to be hopeful, we are often dangerously inclined to focus on reasons associated with our higher intelligence. We identify 'good' reasons with the pursuit of scientific, artistic or political breakthroughs, or with a devotion to God, justice or reputation. However noble such ideals may be, they are also at the mercy of large-scale forces that are hard to command or predict – and as such they may let us down suddenly, leaving us cut off from hope and any sense of why we should continue.

Reblochon cheese has been produced since the 13th century in the Thônes valley of the Aravis massif in south-eastern France. It's a washed-rind, smear-ripened cheese made from raw cow's milk from the Abondance, Montbéliarde and Tarine breeds. It is excellent baked in gratins but comes into its own when cut thickly and spread across fresh baguette. The flavour is at once delicate and tantalising, willing you on to eat a little more in order to gain full mastery over its promise.

As we bite into our baguette and reblochon, we still know, on a rational level, that everything is a disaster. Our reputation is still ruined, people remain unforgiving and the mess will not be sorted out any time soon. And yet, miraculously, these same facts no longer have quite the hold on us they once did. We watch them through a thick pane of glass.

A secure life is one in which we can keep in mind the many reasons to exist that nimbly bypass our centres of logic, and bring them to the fore at moments of crisis. It is a life in which we can fully remember and honour the power of hot baths, cypress trees, lemon soles, capers, figs, dancing, cashmere blankets, hazelnuts, dark chocolate and the sound of crickets. These nonintellectual sources of delight function as thin but infinitely tough ropes that can hold us safely over the gorge of sadness and despair.

When we have done all the thinking we are capable of, we should ensure that there will always be a large slice of soft French cheese to hand, to stand protectively between us and our inclinations to give up.

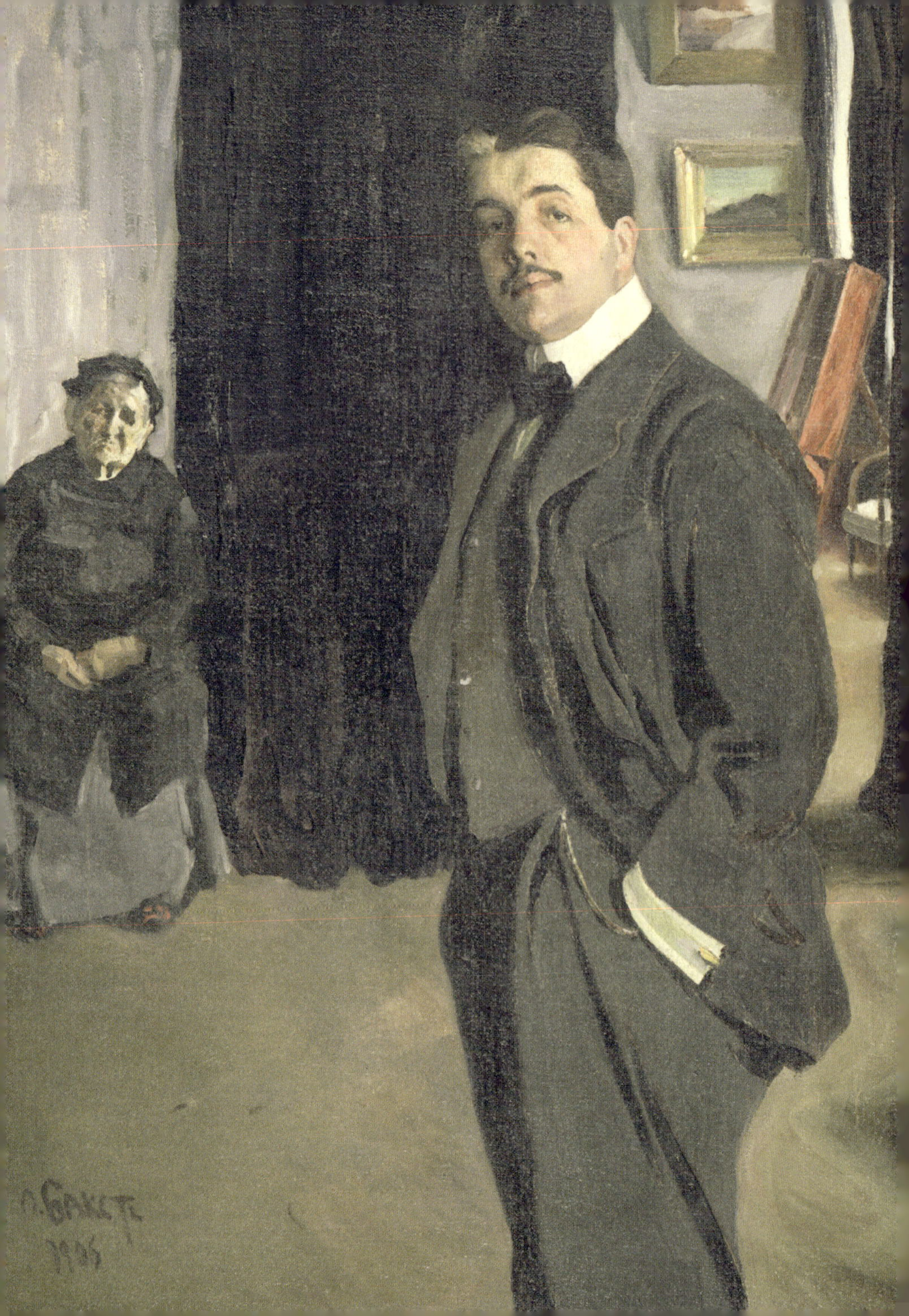

VII.

Affection rather than understanding

Léon Bakst, *Portrait of Sergei Pavlovich Diaghilev with his Nurse*, 1906 (detail). It could be one of the most intelligent decisions we make to recognise the power of simple companionship.

Sergei Diaghilev and his nanny

One of the reasons why we may end up lonelier than we should is because we cling on to a hope that one day, someone will finally fully understand us. With such an elevated ambition in mind, we reject a host of disappointing candidates, take repeated offence at how patchily we are being heard, get into arguments with people who appear obtuse and wilfully ignorant, go to a lot of boring parties and dinners – and long for a person whom we can clearly imagine but never seem to run into.

Sergei Diaghilev was one of the most intelligent and creative minds of the early 20th century. Born in Russia in 1872, his interests ranged from art to physics, psychology to ballet. He began his career organising large exhibitions that introduced new Russian art to the public, then became a director of the imperial theatres, and eventually he founded probably the most influential ballet company in history, the Ballets Russes, which travelled around Europe transforming music, art, costume design, fashion and literature. Diaghilev championed the work of Stravinsky, collaborated with Picasso, employed and had a love affair with Nijinsky, introduced Joyce to Proust and put on versions of *Le Pavillon d'Armide*, *Une Nuit d'Egypte* and *Les Sylphides* that altered the history of the performing arts.

Alongside his work, for a long time, Diaghilev searched for love. He pursued many of his male dancers, his secretary and his librettist, as well as a range of talented choreographers. Yet he could never unite his complicated needs and ideas with those of another – and his love affairs all ended in acrimony.

Eventually though, Diaghilev arrived at a solution to the problems of isolation. He had been looked after since the age of 1 by a nanny called Avdotya from a small village near the Ural Mountains. On the face of it, Diaghilev and Avdotya had nothing in common. She was uneducated, cared nothing for ballet, read almost nothing and hated modern art. Nevertheless, despite a total gulf in intellectual understanding, she and Diaghilev got along very well. They liked to chat about the meals she cooked for him, they discussed their health (hers was robust, his fragile), they were both interested in animals, they went for small walks and they adored playing Scrabble. Recognising the power of their companionship, Diaghilev decided to invite his nanny to be with him all the time as he travelled around Russia and Europe; he took her to important dinners, she was at every one of his rehearsals and she was in the room when impresarios and statesmen dropped in to pay homage and discuss new projects. When the artist and scene designer Léon Bakst was commissioned to paint a portrait of Diaghilev, it seemed natural to include Avdotya in the picture.

It is unlikely that we will have the talent or intellectual range of Diaghilev, but we may well have a version of his dilemma. There are sure to be many things we would like to be understood for: our parents, the character of our ambitions, our political sympathies and hatreds, our feelings about our friends, our relationship to sport, science and art, our sexuality and our sense of humour. It's an edifying list, but one guaranteed to leave us isolated and disconsolate along the way.

Very few people are ever liable to be able to sympathise with us across the board. Sooner or later, everyone – however apparently on our wavelength – will diverge from our tastes and offend our unique perspectives. But with Diaghilev's example in mind, we would be foolish to give up on people simply because they don't understand much about who we happen to be. The point is ultimately not whether our souls mesh perfectly (they never will) but whether two people can be kind to one another on their journey through life. It is affection, not flawless understanding, that we should be seeking in order to defend ourselves against our sorrows.

Once we have a clearer and narrower sense of what a connection with others might be truly about, we will be liberated to enjoy a great many more people, for sympathy and kindness are always in far greater supply than spiritual congruence. There are more individuals who will be ready to cry with us about our difficulties than who will agree with us on how to stage *Boris Godunov*.

Diaghilev was an exceptionally intelligent man, but he was never more so than in realising the limits of intrapersonal understanding. We have looked out for soulmates long enough and hurt enough people along the way in doing so. Now might be the time to seek out a far more plausible candidate: someone with whom we love to chat about what to have for supper, who knows just what to say when we're sad and who is always on hand for a game or two of Scrabble.

LLAMADAS
NACIONALES
INTERNACIONALES
LOCALES - CELULARES
MEGA BURGUER
INTERNET
Sabroso

VIII.

Elsewhere

There is always an elsewhere. There is always Titicaca Street, La Paz, Bolivia.

La Paz, Bolivia

At home, things have gone wrong for us. We have annoyed some important people; we have exhausted the patience of kind acquaintances; when our name comes up in conversation, there are sighs or embarrassed silences. Our failure is common knowledge, and the normal responses are condemnation, laughter and (sometimes) a touch of pity. It might be a relatively big place, but it feels like a village; it seems there will be whispers about us until the day we die.

When the world feels oppressive and narrow, we need to retain a concept – apparently geographical but really existential in nature – of an 'elsewhere'. We must keep in mind the knowledge that there remain places on earth where nothing is known of us, where no one would recognise us, where the concerns are different and where people judge matters in other ways. In our circumstances, otherness isn't merely exotic; it's a promise of less punishing perspectives on our fate. It is a lifeline.

Take, for example, La Paz, the capital of Bolivia, a high, landlocked nation that lacks many of the more obvious tourist attractions of its neighbours and that takes its name from Simón Bolívar, the Venezuelan leader of the

Spanish American war of independence. You may never have been to La Paz, but in claustrophobic moments it could be helpful to become supremely interested in the city home to 800,000 people, 3,600 metres up in the Andean plateau, in the shadow of the perennially snow-capped peaks of the Illimani mountain. You might look up photos of the Plaza España, from where one can catch the cable car down to the neighbourhood of Irpavi, looking out over houses and spacious avenues along the way. You can read about the Aymara indigenous people, who used to run the Inca Empire and who now make up about 40 per cent of the population, their traditional dress of bowler hats, colourful shawls and wide embroidered skirts seen throughout town. You can wander in your imagination along the main marketplace, the Mercado 16 de Julio, or have a moment of refuge in front of a bleeding Christ in the Basílica Nuestra Señora de La Paz. In the Plaza Pérez Velasco, you could snack on some buñuelos, fritters flavoured with cinnamon, while listening to a sombre-faced man playing a plaintive song about lost love by Ernesto Cavour on a charangón.

If things were to come to a head, if the gossip never stopped and our spirits could not lift, then perhaps we really would pack our bags and start again. We could take a small room overlooking a courtyard with eucalyptus trees in the La Casona Hotel on the Avenida Mariscal Santa Cruz, learn Spanish, become a regular in the modestly priced Doña Remedios restaurant off Montevideo Avenue (where they make excellent salteña, an oven-baked empanada containing chicken, peas, potatoes, olives and eggs), read of the latest wranglings in the Asamblea Legislativa Plurinacional in the pages of *El Diario* – and leave the past behind.

We can have different, new lives within one life. We do not have to remain where we are. There is always an elsewhere. There is always La Paz, waiting for us, high in the Andes.

麒麟圖

永樂十二年歲次甲午秋九月榜葛剌國進貢

IX.

Wonder

Unknown artist (formerly attributed to Shen Du), *Tribute Giraffe with Attendant*, 16th century. We should remind ourselves of the wonder of the giraffe when the world becomes familiar and stale.

The emperor's giraffe

One reason we may be sad is because we think we know it all – because everything has grown stale and familiar, and we have (for very understandable reasons) lost the ability to wonder.

Yet the world is always stranger and more unexpected than we can bring ourselves to believe in our dejected moods. Zhu Di (known as Yongle), the third emperor of the Ming dynasty, who ruled from 1402 to 1424, had by middle age grown weary of his role as royal intermediary between heaven and earth; he had a thousand mistresses, he'd conquered Vietnam and tamed the Mongols and he'd commissioned the largest encyclopaedia ever written, the *Yongle Dadian*, which explained every element in the history of Chinese civilisation. But, weary in his soul, the Yongle emperor made a move that none of his predecessors had ever attempted. He sent some ships to explore the wider world. Chinese rulers knew their country to be the most interesting and blessed on the planet and therefore generally felt no need to go elsewhere, beyond subduing a near neighbour. But the emperor asked his explorer and mariner, the eunuch Admiral Zheng He, to go out and make a thorough survey of all the barbarian lands he could find. With a more or less unlimited budget, Zheng He had a vast fleet built in the Longjiang shipyard near Nanjing, and after a banquet presided over by the emperor at which sacrifices were made to Tianfei, the patron Goddess of sailors, China's largest ever expeditionary force set off. It dropped in on Brunei, Java, Thailand, Ceylon (modern-day Sri Lanka) and India, then went over to Arabia and Africa, stopping at Hormuz, Lasa (modern-day Lhasa), Aden, Mogadishu, Brava, Zhubu and Malindi.

Along the way, the admiral picked up a panoply of gifts and treasures that he hoped would amuse and delight the emperor: manuscripts, sculptures, clothes, gold, palm and date trees, figs, all manner of spices, a few slaves and many new concubines. But what the Yongle emperor really loved were animals, and Zheng He picked up a veritable zooful that had never been seen before in China: lions, leopards, dromedary camels, ostriches, zebras, a rhino and antelopes. The emperor was enamoured with one animal in particular: a giraffe that his admiral had picked up from a couple of intrepid Kenyan traders in eastern India. Laying eyes on it for the first time, he stroked the animal's hide, marvelled at its long neck and its graceful but slightly awkward way of walking, and gave it his blessing. His spirits having lifted, the Yongle emperor invited the entire court to take a look. He had an enclosure specially built for the giraffe in his palace and often took walks with it around the grounds. Unsurprisingly, he asked his artist, Shen Du, to capture his new friend – an honour he did not bestow on any other foreign animal.

We probably all experienced some of the Yongle emperor's excitement when we first laid eyes on a giraffe. We, too, would have marvelled at that long neck and admired the bright patterning and strange gait. But somewhere along the line, we stopped wondering – about giraffes, and pretty much everything else as well. The world became familiar and then stale.

Perhaps we should not have given up so easily. Giraffes remain hugely odd and importantly wonderful. We do not live on a dull planet; we have merely allowed our sorrows to drain our capacity for joy. When depression weighs us down, we should strive to remind ourselves that the world remains full of giraffes, and what they symbolise: renewed charm and creativity, new opportunities for interest and fresh reasons to keep going.

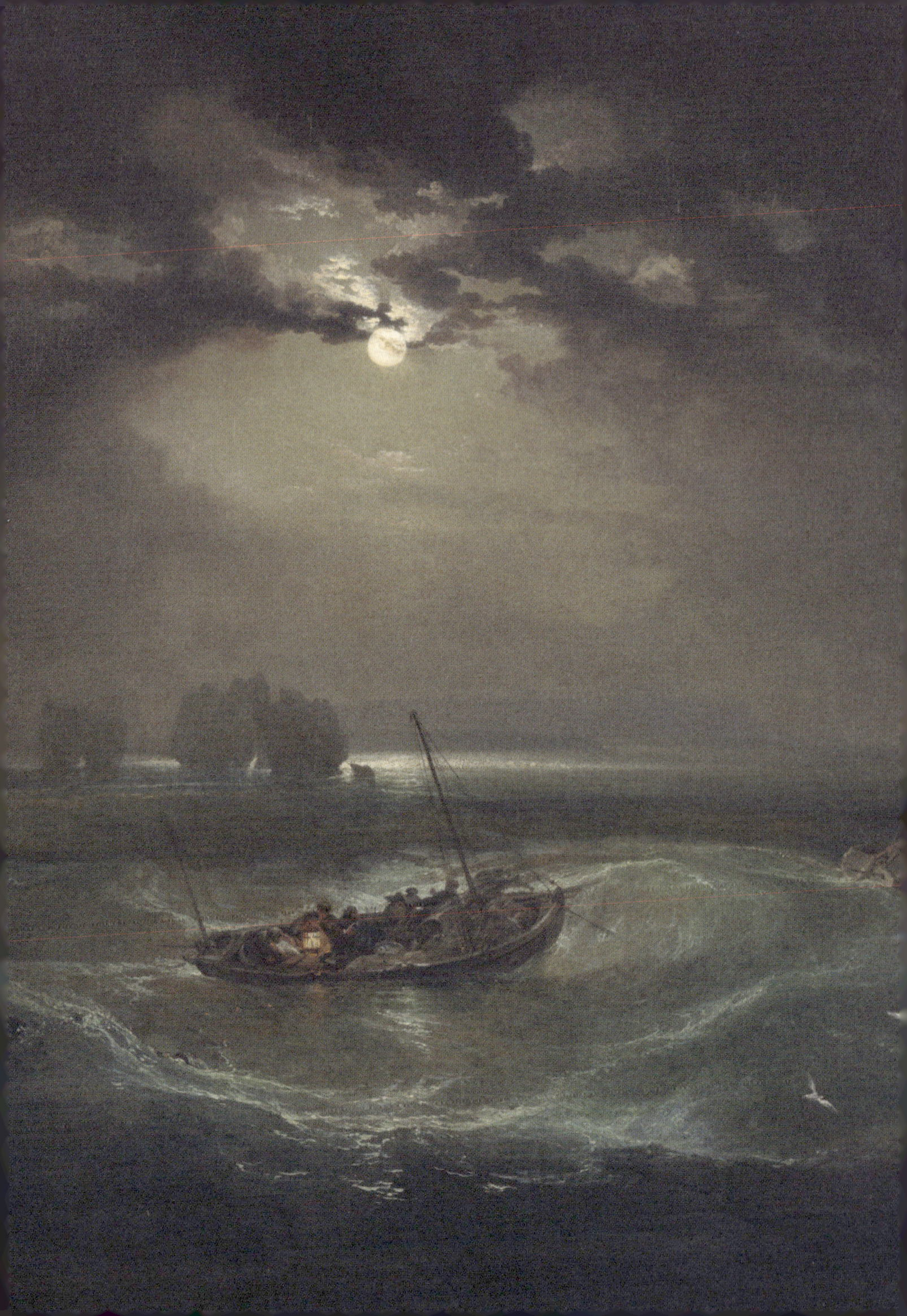

X.

The promise of dawn

Joseph Mallord William Turner, *Fishermen at Sea*, exhibited 1796 (detail).
No critical conclusions can be drawn between dusk and dawn.

J.M.W. Turner and sunrise

It's been a long and difficult day; it's late, but we can't sleep. In the dark hours, as so often happens, our worries close in. Our minds are filled with sickening memories of the stupid things we did yesterday and we drown in fearful anticipation of the looming troubles of tomorrow. We feel swamped, inadequate and exhausted.

Our mental condition at such times could be visualised in one of the earliest works of the English artist J.M.W. Turner, *Fishermen at Sea*, painted when he was still in his early 20s.

A frail boat is at the mercy of a stormy swell; submerged rocks could be anywhere, invisible in the gloom. For a moment, the moon emerges from behind the clouds, only to cast confusing, eerie shadows; why did they even set out on such a night? Catastrophe could strike at any moment. For Turner, the night was always a time of supreme fear.

In one of his grandest paintings from the middle of his career, Turner summons the sense of dread that must have been felt when the avenging forces of the Carthaginian warlord Hannibal made their way through the Alps at night,

Joseph Mallord William Turner, *Snow Storm: Hannibal and his Army Crossing the Alps*, exhibited 1812

towards the defenceless cities of Italy. Turner was no scholar, and it was not the historical details that concerned him. Rather, he tapped into something universal: the way that, in the dark, fears intensify into terror.

For hundreds of thousands of years, night was a time of maximal vulnerability, when unseen predators or enemies could get close. Paradoxically, we survived by stoking our worries: every odd sound had to be imagined as a mortal threat or we might die from complacency. Later, to encourage them to stay safely in bed, children were told of sinister, malign beings that emerged only at midnight. Those who were terrified in the dark had an incomparably better chance of making it to the next day.

We ourselves are not going to be devoured by a lion and we don't believe in witches or goblins, but we've inherited a posture of fear: at night our minds are primed for dread.

It was perhaps because he was so sensitised to this psychological tendency that in later life Turner became increasingly obsessed with depicting the dawn.

Turner was drawn to Switzerland, where from the window of his boarding house at Interlaken he could look out in the early morning and see, across the still water, the steep

Joseph Mallord William Turner, *The Blue Rigi, Sunrise*, 1842

granite cliffsides of Mount Rigi gradually emerging in the sunlight. Although we now take it for granted and rarely witness it, dawn was for our ancestors a powerfully important phenomenon and a logical object of quasi-religious reverence: the nocturnal predators had gone, colour was returning to the world, the shapes of things were growing solid and they could scan the horizon and anticipate what was to come.

It's not that the return of the sun can truly solve all our problems, but it possesses an important symbolic power to dissipate the additional layer of dread which, thanks to our evolutionary history, envelops us at night.

In an especially evocative work, *Sunrise with Sea Monsters*, which he never exhibited during his lifetime, Turner targeted precisely this idea.

As dawn breaks over the sea, the ill-defined, monstrous shapes that we can only just make out in the lower-middle of the picture seem to dissolve. They are retreating to the backs of our minds, leaving the more rational and practical aspects of our nature to come to the fore.

Joseph Mallord William Turner, *Sunrise with Sea Monsters*, c. 1845

Joseph Mallord William Turner, *Dawn after the Wreck*, c. 1841

Perhaps Turner's most poignant work, created close to the end of his long life, is *Dawn after the Wreck*. The painting depicts the morning after a merciless night. We imagine the ship pulverised against the rocks. Now the lonely dog wails by the shore for its lost master, drowned in the swell. The trouble hasn't gone, but there's no longer a sense of panic. The mood is solemn and sad, but the moment of terror has passed. Despite everything, life will continue.

Turner is our guide to a crucial thought that modern technical sophistication leads us to forget: we underestimate the degree to which our distress may depend not simply on the actual gravity of a situation but, additionally, on the presence or absence of daylight. It seems such a trivial element: the mere passage of a few hours, the spinning of the planet that will direct our portion of the Earth back towards the Sun. Yet its effect on us is profound. Our minds have been shaped by the long history of human experience. Our desperation, in the dark, isn't the final word on our condition – we must never try to reach any critical conclusions between dusk and dawn. We must wait until daylight returns, and with it – if we are lucky – a semblance of composure and a new sense of imagination for our future.

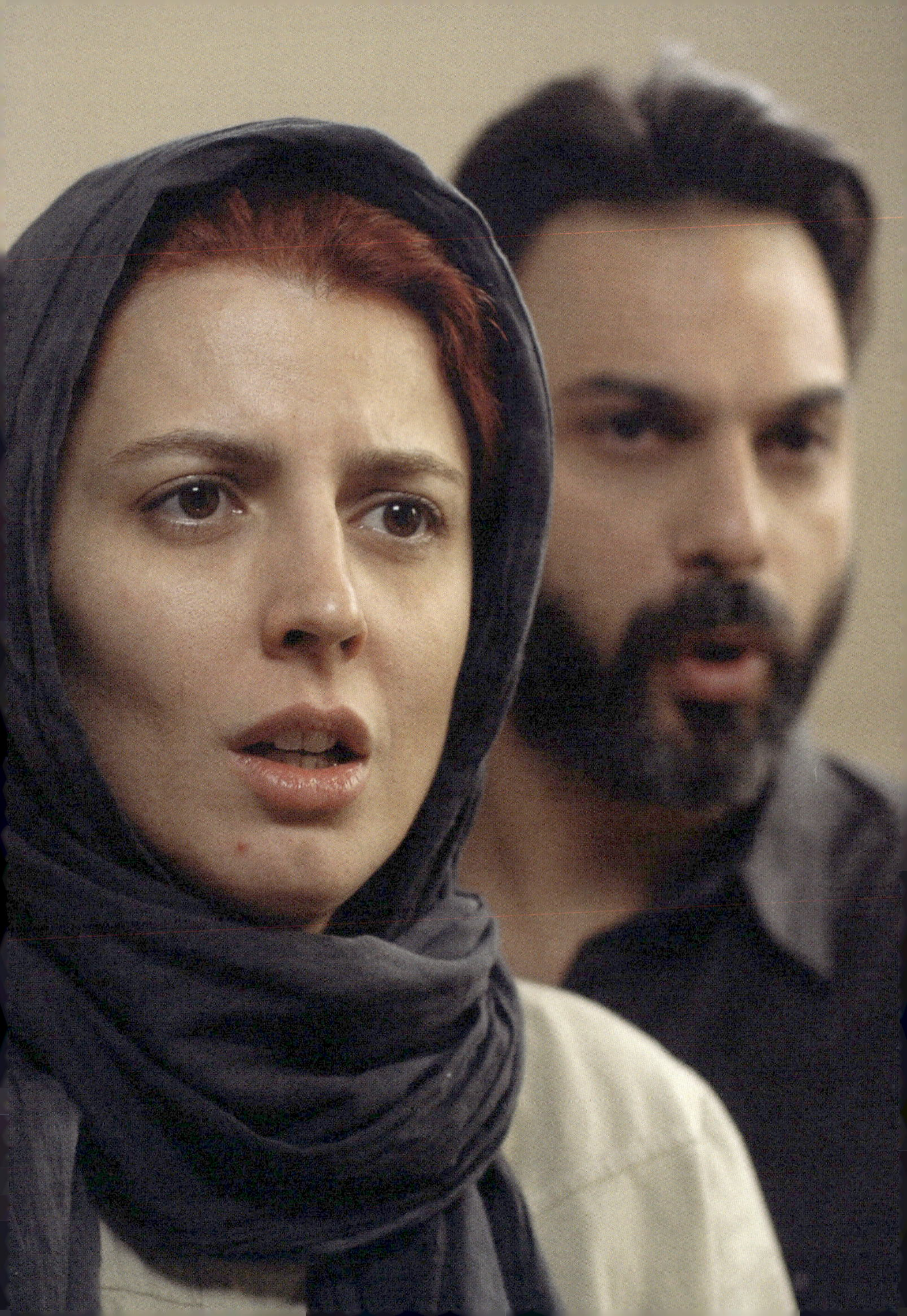

XI.

Good escapism

Still from Asghar Farhadi's film *A Separation*, 2011.
Cinema can provide us with some of our finest possibilities to 'escape'.

Iranian cinema

Few people are more likely to attract our disdain than those we deem to be 'escapists'. Rather than standing firm and confronting the sources of their distress, these renegades give their problems free rein by running directly away from them. They combine two of the most seemingly objectionable psychological traits: cowardice and laziness.

But whether such tough judgement is ultimately deserved comes down to what problems we are talking about. There are certain issues that, by virtue of their intractability, are truly unlikely ever to be resolved – and which therefore we might well be permitted to flee without meriting condemnation for doing so.

It truly is 'escaping' in the bad sense when we neglect to work for our exams and play video games instead, or neglect household chores and replace them with porn, or evade emotional or physical troubles that could be solved by seeking out a therapist or doctor. But it hardly constitutes 'escapism' to try to find some distance after the death of a child, a declaration of bankruptcy or receiving a fatal diagnosis. We are not, in such circumstances, in any danger of evading a necessary confrontation with pain.

There is no amount of work we might do, but are choosing not to do, to overcome our difficulties; we are simply seeking a little respite from insistent suffering. We are trying to find the courage to carry on.

Part of the opprobrium heaped on escapism comes from the way people characteristically choose to escape: with heroin and crack cocaine, opioids and benzodiazepines, too much vodka and Sancerre. In other words, via escape hatches that may destroy our minds and bodies and can cause no end of difficulties for those who depend on us.

There are, however, other equally powerful but less destructive ways in which we might run away for a while. This might be by becoming wholly absorbed in the history of another country, in the development of the garden or the kitchen, or in physical exercise or the life of a pet – all conduits to becoming, for a few hours and without causing any ill effects, no longer just a person who has lost a child, ruined their business or unleashed a scandal.

We might, for example, become deeply engrossed in the history of Iranian cinema, beginning with some of the early prerevolutionary masterpieces like *Lor Girl*, *A Party in Hell*, *Qeysar*, *Dar Emtedade Shab*, *Amir Arsalan* or *Ganj-e Qarun*. Gripped by the subtle sensibility and aesthetic ambition, we might move on to the Iranian New Wave and its two high points: Nasser Taghvai's *Tranquility in the Presence of Others* and Bahram Beyzai's *Downpour*. We might read up about the Khomeini government's surprising decision in 1981 to increase the funding of film schools, the annual Fajr International Film Festival and the Farabi Cinema Foundation, which gave rise to a whole generation of fresh talent. Then we would be able to delve into the work of directors like Asghar Farhadi, Jafar Panahi and Hana Makhmalbaf – and, depending on our tastes, we might fall a little in love with the actors Pantea Bahram, Mitra Hajjar or Payman Maadi.

This cultural seam might keep us profoundly occupied for a thousand hours or more. Over the months, our thoughts would no longer need to bump into every sharp edge of the mind. Especially in the evenings, we would have something to insulate us against yet another confrontation with a sadness that can never be 'solved'.

Then, when done, we could with equal energy move on to Chilean poetry or the traditions of European monasticism, the music of Pergolesi or the clothes of a small Belgian fashion brand. We could go through phases of absorption in Venetian glass-making or Hopi textiles, Nigerian dance or life at the court of Louis XIV.

Once we start to take escapism with the seriousness it merits, there is no limit to the all-consuming avenues we might follow in culture, sociology, politics, nutrition, fashion or housework. We need never be wholly alone with our suffering again.

The idea of mastery over problems is over-privileged. Many problems simply aren't amenable to fixing, and so a sound life requires that we become experts not just in self-exploration and confrontation, but also – especially after trouble has struck – in selective denial and distraction, and the rare and under-appreciated virtue of knowing how to think exclusively about something else for a while.

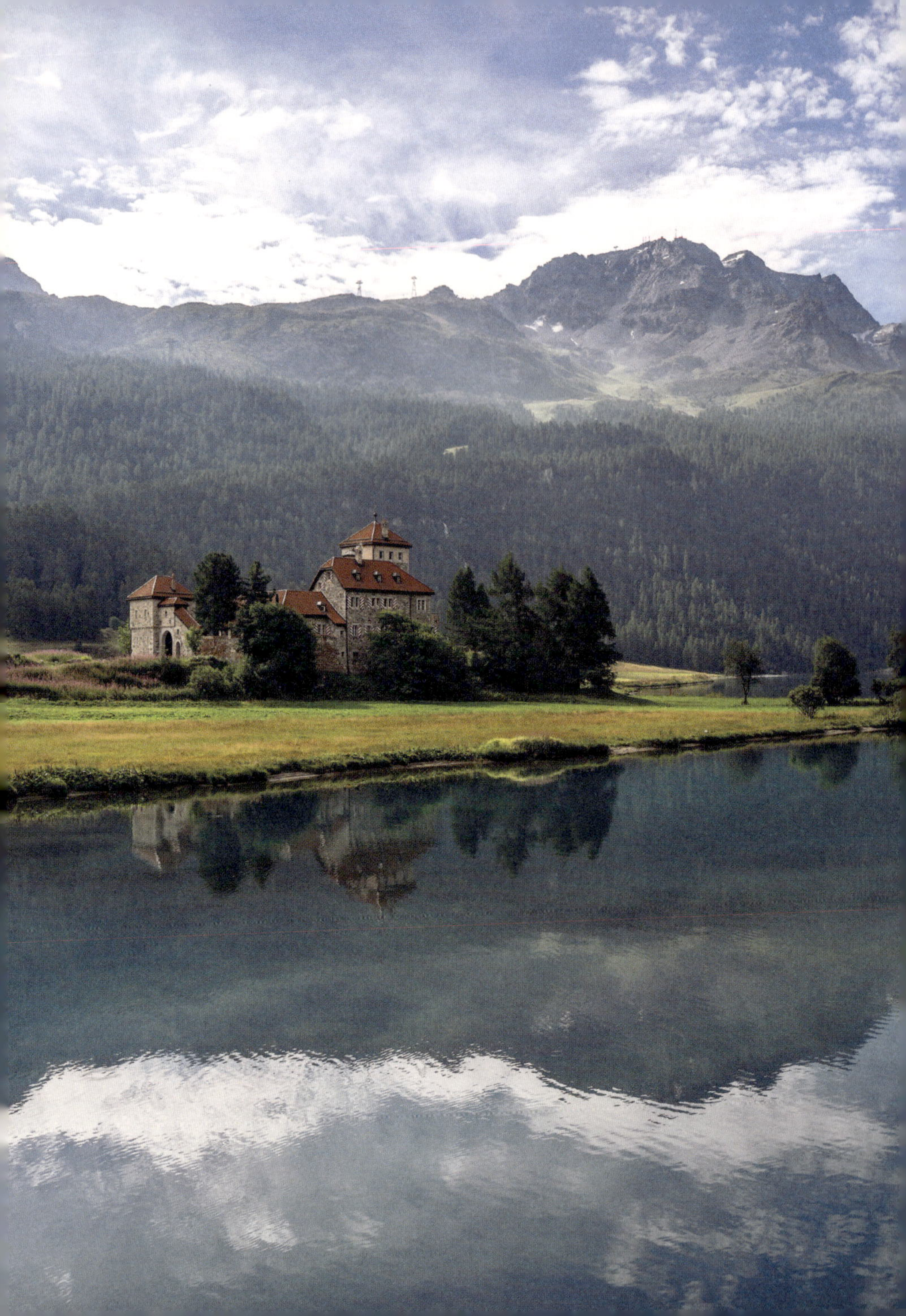

XII.

Acceptance

Nietzsche became compelled by the idea of *amor fati* – the realisation that life is a web of consequences that we are powerless to alter at will – on one of his walks around Lake Silvaplana, Upper Engadine, Switzerland.

Nietzsche and *amor fati*

One of the strangest yet most intriguing aspects of Friedrich Nietzsche's ideas is his repeated enthusiasm for a concept that he called *amor fati*, translated from Italian as 'a love of one's fate' – or, to expand, a resolute, enthusiastic acceptance of everything that has happened in one's life. A person who welcomes amor fati doesn't seek to erase anything of their past, but rather accepts what has occurred, the good and the bad, the mistaken and the wise, with strength and an all-embracing gratitude that borders on enthusiasm.

This refusal to regret the past is heralded as a virtue at many points in Nietzsche's work. In his book, *The Gay Science*, written during a period of great personal hardship for the philosopher, Nietzsche writes:

> I want to learn more and more to see as beautiful what is necessary in things; then I shall be one of those who makes things beautiful. Amor fati: let that be my love henceforth! I do not want to wage war against what is ugly. I do not want to accuse; I do not even want to accuse those who accuse. Looking away shall be my only negation. And all in all and on the whole: some day I wish to be only a Yes-sayer.

A few years later, in *Ecce Homo*, Nietzsche writes: 'My formula for greatness in a human being is amor fati: that one wants nothing to be different, not forward, not backward, not in all eternity. Not merely bear what is necessary, still less conceal it ... but love it.'

In most areas of life, most of the time, we do the very opposite. We kick violently against negative events and do not accept their role in our biographies. We do not love or embrace painful lessons. We spend a large amount of time taking stock of our errors, regretting and lamenting the unfortunate turns of fate and wishing that things could have gone differently. We are typically mighty opponents of anything that smacks of resignation or fatalism. We want to alter and improve things – ourselves, politics, the economy, the course of history – and part of this means refusing to be passive about the errors, injustices and ugliness of our own and the collective past. Nietzsche himself, in some moods, knew this defiance full well. There was much emphasis in his work on action, initiative and self-assertion.

However, it is one of the beautiful aspects of Nietzsche's thinking that he is aware that in order to lead a good life, we need to keep in mind plenty of opposing ideas and marshal them as and when they become relevant.

In Nietzsche's eyes, we don't need to be consistent; we need to have the ideas to hand that can salve our wounds. He isn't, therefore, asking us to choose between a glorious fatalism on the one hand or a vigorous willing on the other. He is allowing us to have recourse to either intellectual move depending on the occasion. He wishes our mental toolkit to have more than one set of ideas: to have, as it were, both a hammer and a saw.

In Nietzsche's own life, there was much that he had tried to change and overcome. He had fled his restrictive family in Germany and escaped to the Swiss Alps; he had tried to get away from the narrowness of academia and become a freelance writer; he had tried to find a wife who could be both a lover and an intellectual soulmate. But a lot in this project of self-creation and self-overcoming had gone very wrong. He couldn't get his family, especially his mother and sister, out of his head. What were, in his eyes, their maddening attitudes and prejudices (anti-Semitism in particular) seemed to have spread across the whole of bourgeois Europe. His books sold dismally, and he was forced to more or less beg from friends and family in order to keep going. Meanwhile, his halting, gauche attempts to seduce women were met with ridicule and rejection. There must have been so many lamentations and regrets running through his mind during his walks across the

Upper Engadine and his nights in his modest wooden chalet in Sils Maria: *If only I had stuck with an academic career, if only I'd been more confident around certain women, if only I'd written in a more popular style, if only I'd been born in France...*

It was precisely because such thoughts (and each of us has our own distinct version of them) can be so destructive and soul-sapping that the idea of amor fati grew compelling to Nietzsche. Amor fati was the idea that he needed in order to regain sanity after hours of self-recrimination and criticism. It's the idea we ourselves may need at 4 a.m. to finally quieten a mind that has started gnawing into itself shortly after midnight. It's an idea with which a troubled spirit can greet the first signs of dawn.

At the height of amor fati, we recognise that things really could not have been otherwise, because everything we are and have done is bound closely together in a web of consequences that began with our birth, which we are powerless to alter at will. We see that what went right and what went wrong are as one, and we commit ourselves to accepting both and to no longer destructively hoping that things could have been otherwise. The fact is that we were headed to a degree of catastrophe from the start. We can understand why we are the desperately imperfect beings we are and why we had to mess things up as badly as we did. In this moment of clarity we can say to ourselves, with mingled tears of grief and ecstasy, a resounding 'yes' to the whole of life, in its agony and its occasional moments of awesome beauty.

In a letter to a friend written in the summer of 1882, Nietzsche tried to sum up the new spirit of acceptance that he had learnt to lean on to protect him from his agony: 'I am in a mood of fatalistic "surrender to God" – I call it amor fati, so much so, that I would be willing to rush into a lion's jaws.'

And that is where, after too much regret, we should learn sometimes to join him.

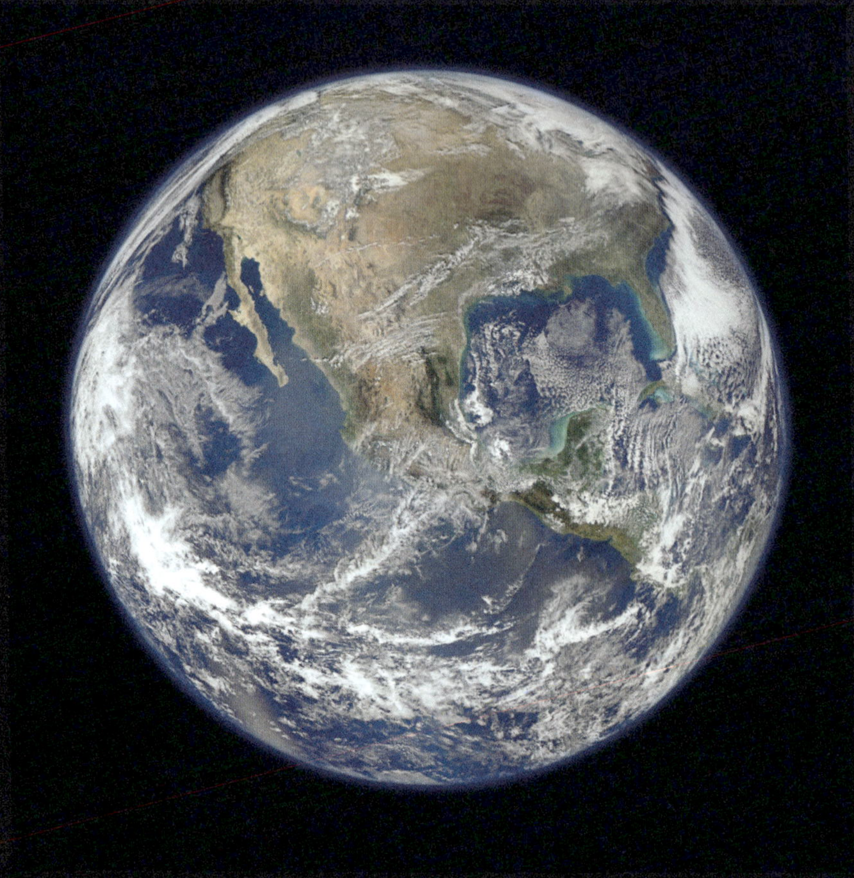

XIII.

Future reasons to be hopeful

Blue Marble Earth created by the Suomi NPP satellite. We must face the future with radical open-mindedness and remind ourselves that we do not know what lies ahead.

One of the reasons we may decide *not* to keep living is because we feel we know the rest. We may not claim to know the future in detail, but we do feel we know it in its broadest outlines – and that is why we feel sure we don't want to go on any more. The years ahead are going to contain further pain, setbacks, hatred, shame, disgrace and viciousness. And we have, understandably, had enough.

The role this certainty about the future plays in sinking our mood suggests that in order to keep faith with life, something very important needs to take place in our minds: we have to stop feeling that we know what lies ahead. We must give up our claims to eternal omniscience and accept that just as we had no idea what was coming to us a few years back, neither can we hope to know where we will be four or five summers from now.

An attitude of fundamental doubt might seem like a way to give an advantage to despair, but more fairly viewed, it is a route to a necessary and redemptive kind of scepticism, in which hope is at last given a fair chance to grow.

Of course, we can't rule out yet more horror. But nor, for that matter, can we rule out an eventual upside. There is no definitive reason why our health might not recover, why the outer world (that took such a turn for the worse) might not slowly become more benevolent, why a new way of looking at issues might not arise or why something very good that we can't even presently imagine might not one day show up.

To despair is to claim to know everything. To decide to end our life is to assume that we are able, from one point in time, to envision the way things will be until the end of our natural days. This isn't just hubris and tragedy, it is intellectual folly.

The only honest position is to face the future with radical open-mindedness. We can't and don't know what is coming. Therefore, a primary reason to carry on is the hope of eventually stumbling on further, unexpected reasons to be hopeful. We must banish our despairing surety about what is ahead – the future version of ourselves may look back on who we are right now and beseech us to keep faith with the journey. We can't know now about the years to come, and for that reason alone, we must give ourselves every generous chance to find out. There will be plenty more reasons to be hopeful; our list is only just starting.

Illustration list

P. 12 Mark Rothko, *Red on Maroon*, 1959, on display in the galleries at Tate Britain, London. Photo Sam Mellish/Alamy Stock Photo. Artwork © 1998 Kate Rothko Prizel & Christopher Rothko ARS, NY and DACS, London

P. 15 Mark Rothko, *Red on Maroon*, 1959. Oil paint, acrylic paint and glue tempera on canvas, 266.7 × 238.8 × 3.5 cm. Tate, London. © 1998 Kate Rothko Prizel & Christopher Rothko ARS, NY and DACS, London

P. 20 Human head and brain. Magnetic resonance imaging (MRI) scan of a midsagittal section through the head of a healthy, 37-year-old female patient, showing structures of the brain, intracerebral arteries, spine and facial tissues. Photo Zephyr/Science Photo Library

P. 28 Sleeping baby. Photo kledge/iStock

P. 33 Rogier van der Weyden, *The Virgin and Child*, 1435–1438. Oil on panel, 100 × 52 cm. Prado, Madrid. Image Copyright Museo Nacional del Prado © Photo MNP/Scala, Florence

P. 36 Metal figure of a porcupine with quills. Made by Franz Bergman factory in Vienna, likely by the artist Karl Fuhrmann, early 20th century. Freud Museum, London. Photo by Nick Cunard/www.nickcunard.co.uk

P. 42 Karl Theodor von Piloty, *The Last Moments of the Girondists*, 1880. Oil on wood, 28 × 44 cm. Formerly Sammlung-Dr.-Georg-Schäfer-Stiftung. Kunsthandel München 1999. Photo akg-images

P. 48 Lucas Cranach the Elder, *The Fountain of Youth*, 1546 (detail). Berlin, Gemäldegalerie – Staatliche Museen zu Berlin (Inv. 593). Oil on wooden panel, 120.6 × 186.1 cm. Photo Jörg P. Anders © 2023. Photo Scala, Florence/bpk, Bildagentur für Kunst, Kulture und Geschichte, Berlin

P. 51 Lucas Cranach the Elder, *The Fountain of Youth*, 1546. Berlin, Gemäldegalerie – Staatliche Museen zu Berlin (Inv. 593). Oil on wooden panel, 120.6 × 186.1 cm. Photo Jörg P. Anders © 2023. Photo Scala, Florence/bpk, Bildagentur für Kunst, Kulture und Geschichte, Berlin

P. 54 Caspar David Friedrich, *Dolmen in the Snow*, 1807 (detail). Oil on canvas, 61 × 80 cm. Dresden, Galerie Neue Meister – Staatliche Kunstsammlungen (Inv.: Gal. Nr. 2196). Photo Jürgen Karpinski. © 2023. Photo Scala, Florence/bpk, Bildagentur für Kunst, Kultur und Geschichte, Berlin

P. 59 Caspar David Friedrich, *The Large Enclosure* (also known as *The Great Preserve*) in Dresden, 1831–1832. Oil on canvas, 73.5 × 102.5 cm. Dresden, Galerie Neue Meister – Staatliche Kunstsammlungen. Photo Jürgen Karpinski. © 2023. Photo Scala, Florence/bpk, Bildagentur für Kunst, Kultur und Geschichte, Berlin

P. 64 The Eiffel Tower. Paris, 1956. Photo by Maurice Zalewski/Corbis via Getty Images

P. 67 Image from p.68 of Hans Vredeman de Vries, *Perspective* (Leiden, 1604), part I, pl. 28. Getty Research Institute, Los Angeles (88-B6279)

P. 70 Astronomer with quadrant observing a meteor. Turkish miniature, Nusrat-Namah, 1584. Gouache on paper. Topkapi Palace Museum Library, Istanbul (Ms Hazine 1365). Photo Roland and Sabrina Michaud/akg-images

P. 74 Macrauchenia. This extinct prehistoric mammal lived 7 million to 20,000 years ago (the Late Miocene to the Late Pleistocene). Illustration by Michael Long/Science Photo Library

P. 80 President Nixon and his daughters, Tricia and Julie, with their children, Christopher Nixon Cox and Jennie Eisenhower. Courtesy of the Richard Nixon Foundation

P. 84 Archaeologists excavating the site of the 'Marlow Warlord', Berkshire. Reproduced with permission of Dr Gabor Thomas, University of Reading

P. 87 'Anglo-Saxon military chief, trumpeter and warriors, Anno 975'. Aquatint from Sir Samuel Rush Meyrick and Charles Hamilton Smith, *The Costume of the Original Inhabitants of the British Islands...* (R. Havell: London, 1815). British Library, London. Photo © British Library Board. All rights reserved/Bridgeman Images

P. 90 Mick Jagger, during filming of *World in Action*, 31st July 1967. Photo ITV/Shutterstock

P. 93 Mick Jagger, during filming of *World in Action*, 31st July 1967. Personal appearance of Mick Jagger, after the quashing of his jail sentence for being in possession of drugs, in which he discusses his attitude towards the society in which he lives with four leaders of the establishment. Photo ITV/Shutterstock

P. 96 Cecil Beaton, *Cyril Connolly*, 1942. Photo Cecil Beaton Studio Archive © Conde Nast

P. 100 Turquoise mosaic skull representing the god Tezcatlipoca, c. 1400–1521. Turquoise and lignite mosaic on a human skull, 19 × 12.2 × 13.9 cm. British Museum, London. Photo © The Trustees of the British Museum, London

P. 106 Gloria Gaynor, 1979. Photo Richard E. Aaron/Redferns/Getty Images

P. 112 Kobayashi Kiyochika, *Fireflies at Ochanomizu*, c. 1880 (detail). Colour woodblock print, 24 × 35 cm. Photograph © 2023 Museum of Fine Arts, Boston. All rights reserved/William Sturgis Bigelow Collection/Bridgeman Images

P. 118 Berlin's Potsdamer Platz as seen from Café Josty, 1930. Mary Evans/Süddeutsche Zeitung Photo

P. 126 Titanic's port-side A-Deck promenade. Photo taken by Francis Browne SJ, 11th April 1912 © Fr Browne SJ Collection

P. 132 Albrecht Dürer, *Six Studies of Pillows* (verso), 1493. Pen and brown ink, 27.8 × 20.2 cm. Metropolitan Museum of Art, New York, Robert Lehman Collection, 1975 (Acc. 1975.1.862)

P. 135 Albrecht Dürer, *Self-portrait, Study of a Hand and a Pillow* (recto), 1493. Pen and brown ink, 27.8 × 20.2 cm. Metropolitan Museum of Art, New York, Robert Lehman Collection, 1975 (Acc. 1975.1.862)

P. 138 Albrecht Dürer, *Columbine*, 1495–1500. Watercolour and opaque paint on parchment, 35.5 × 28.7 cm. The Albertina Museum, Vienna

P. 140 Albrecht Dürer, *Triumphal Arch*, c. 1515. Woodcut, 45.7 × 62.2 cm. Metropolitan Museum of Art, New York, Harris Brisbane Dick Fund, 1928 (Acc. 28.82.7–.42)

P. 142 Albrecht Dürer, *The Four Horsemen, from the Apocalypse*, 1498. Woodcut, 38.7 × 27.9 cm. Metropolitan Museum of Art, New York, Gift of Junius Spencer Morgan, 1919, 19.73.209

P. 143 Albrecht Dürer, *Portrait of the Artist with a Thistle Flower*, 1493. Painting, 56 × 44 cm. Paris, Louvre (Inv.: RF2382). Photo Tony Querrec. © 2023. RMN-Grand Palais /Dist. Photo Scala, Florence

P. 146 Georg Friedrich Kersting, *Embroiderer*, 1817. Oil on board, 59 × 49 cm. National Museum, Warsaw

P. 152 Georg Friedrich Kersting, *Young Woman Sewing by Lamplight*, 1823. Oil on canvas, 40.3 × 34.2 cm. Munich, Neue Pinakothek München – Bayerische Staatsgemäldesammlungen. © 2023. Photo Scala, Florence/bpk, Bildagentur für Kunst, Kultur und Geschichte, Berlin

P. 154 Georg Friedrich Kersting, *Man Reading by Lamplight*, 1814. Oil on canvas, 47.5 × 37 cm. Kunst Museum Winterthur, Stiftung Oskar Reinhart. Photo © SIK-ISEA, Zürich (Philipp Hitz)

P. 156 Constantin Hansen, *A Group of Danish Artists in Rome*, 1837 (detail). Oil on canvas, 62 × 74 cm. SMK (Statens Museum for Kunst), National Gallery of Denmark, Copenhagen

P. 160 Constantin Hansen, *A Group of Danish Artists in Rome*, 1837. Oil on canvas, 62 × 74 cm. SMK (Statens Museum for Kunst), National Gallery of Denmark, Copenhagen

P. 164 George Jones (attr.), *Banquet in the Thames Tunnel*, c. 1827. Oil on board, 37.5 × 32.5 cm. Ironbridge Gorge Museum, Telford, Shropshire. Photo © Ironbridge Gorge Museum/ Bridgeman Images

P. 168 Canaletto (Giovanni Antonio Canal), *View of the Entrance to the Arsenal, Venice*, 1732–1735. Oil on canvas, 47 × 79 cm. From the Woburn Abbey Collection

P. 170 Handle of the door between hall and salon. Lost (photo from 1972 with original setting). Copyright Archive Leitner. Photo Studio Urban

P. 172 Christian Furr, *Petit Reblochon on Midnight Blue*, 2016 (detail). Oil on wood, 31 × 22 cm. © Christian Furr. All rights reserved 2023/Bridgeman Images

P. 176 Léon Bakst, *Portrait of Sergei Pavlovich Diaghilev with his Nurse*, 1906 (detail). Oil on canvas, 161 × 116 cm. State Russian Museum, St Petersburg, Russia. Photo Bridgeman Images

226

P. 182 Titicaca Street, La Paz, Bolivia. Photo © Pablo Kersz, 2009

P. 188 Unknown artist (formerly attributed to Shen Du), *Tribute Giraffe with Attendant*, 16th century. Ink and colour on silk; mounted as a hanging scroll, 80 × 40.6 cm. Philadelphia Museum of Art, Gift of John T. Dorrance (1977-42-1)

P. 194 Joseph Mallord William Turner, *Fishermen at Sea*, exhibited 1796 (detail). Oil on canvas, 91.4 × 122.2 cm. Tate, London. © Photo Tate

P. 197 Joseph Mallord William Turner, *Snow Storm: Hannibal and his Army Crossing the Alps*, exhibited 1812. Oil on canvas, 146 × 237.5 cm. Tate, London. © Photo Tate

P. 199 Joseph Mallord William Turner, *The Blue Rigi, Sunrise*, 1842. Watercolour on paper, 29.7 × 45 cm. Tate, London. © Photo Tate

P. 201 Joseph Mallord William Turner, *Sunrise with Sea Monsters*, c. 1845. Oil on canvas, 91.4 × 121.9 cm. Tate, London. © Photo Tate

P. 202 Joseph Mallord William Turner, *Dawn after the Wreck*, c. 1841. Pencil, watercolour, body colour, red chalk & scraping on paper, 25.1 × 36.8 cm. The Courtauld, London (Samuel Courtauld Trust). Photo © The Courtauld/Bridgeman Images

P. 204 Still from Asghar Farhadi, *A Separation*, 2011. Photo 12/Alamy Stock Photo

P. 210 Silvaplanersee, Switzerland. Photo Achim Thomae/Getty Images

P. 218 'Blue Marble' Earth. Montage created from photographs taken by the Visible/Infrared Imager Radiometer Suite (VIIRS) instrument on board the Suomi NPP satellite. Photo NASA

The School of Life is a global organisation helping people lead more fulfilled lives. It is a resource for helping us understand ourselves, for improving our relationships, our careers and our social lives – as well as for helping us find calm and get more out of our leisure hours. We do this through films, workshops, books, gifts and community. You can find us online, in stores and in welcoming spaces around the globe.

theschooloflife.com